H. R. H.

PRINCESS
MARGARET

The Younger Sister

Cecil Beaton

Her Royal Highness's favourite portrait

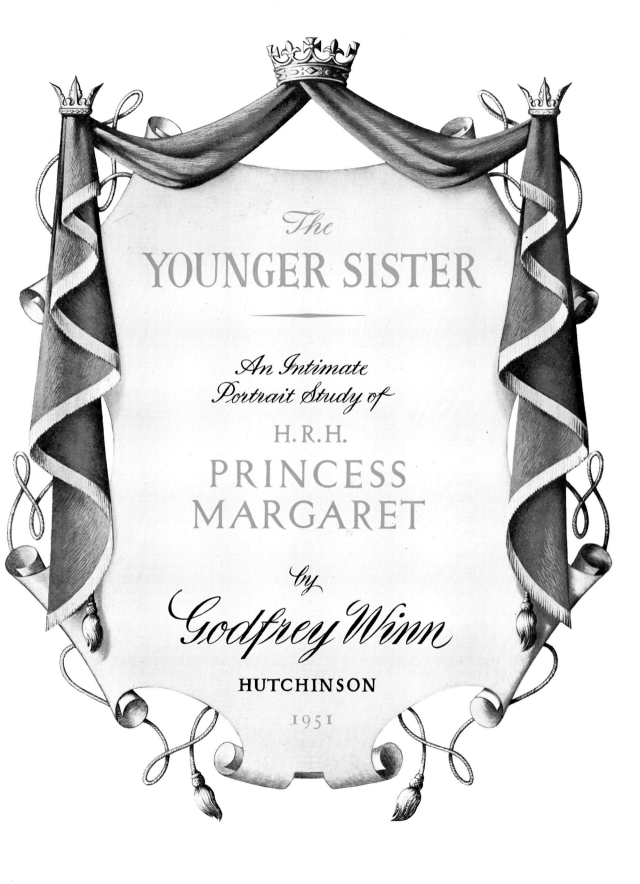

The
YOUNGER SISTER

*An Intimate
Portrait Study of*

H. R. H.
PRINCESS
MARGARET

by

Godfrey Winn

HUTCHINSON

1951

MADE AND PRINTED IN GREAT BRITAIN
BY THE HUTCHINSON PRINTING TRUST, LTD.

DEDICATED

TO ALL

YOUNGER

SISTERS

EVERYWHERE

My grateful thanks are due to Mr. Charles Eade, the editor of the Sunday Dispatch who first commissioned this portrait

August 21st, 1930

S I CAME UP in the lift to the floor at Buckingham Palace where Princess Margaret has her apartments overlooking the courtyard and the Mall I was remembering the last time that I had the opportunity to study the King and Queen's younger daughter at close quarters.

It was the last Christmas of the war. The two Princesses were staging one of their own private pantomimes, in the Waterloo Chamber, at Windsor Castle. I have the programme still. On the outside it says:

"Old Mother Red Riding Boots, devised by Princess Elizabeth, Princess Margaret and Hubert Tannar."

Mr. Tannar was the headmaster of the Royal School at Windsor Park, and when he died not long ago the Princesses lost a dear friend. He was the enthusiastic producer of all their childhood pantomimes, and extremely successful in the way that he persuaded his mixed bag of performers to speak up, to forget their mutual shyness, and also to forget the source of many of their lines of dialogue.

For instance, after the dress rehearsal Princess Margaret rang up her producer and said, "Oh, Mr. Tannar, Papa noticed

Aged two years

Aged three years

that we left out one of his jokes. He thinks it is one of his best ones, too. So please can we put it back again tonight?"

It was put back, and at the performance I attended I noticed that the King and Queen, who were seated just in front of me, led the laughter at all the sallies, making the audience feel that this was a truly happy family party, and that the show should be enjoyed in the spirit of private charades.

Actually, there was one professional performer among them. At least, one member of the cast with a really professional poise and dash. The principal girl, named in the programme as *The Honourable Lucinda Fairfax*. The moment she made her first entrance you felt a quickening of interest, the suspense that only comes in the theatre in the presence of a really important personality.

I can see her now, coming forward to the

Two childhood studies from the

microphone and waiting for the applause to die down before, with a most assured nod to the orchestra, she started her first number. It was called *Sing a Song of Tomorrow Today*. And I remember thinking at the same time what a symbolic title it was because, although Princess Margaret was then only fourteen, it was abundantly clear that here was an embryo "star", already emerging from the chrysalis stage, with all the promise of being a glitteringly attractive butterfly.

Later, when the two sisters sang the duet *Sur le Pont d'Avignon*, somehow you found yourself looking at the younger one. It was the same in the sketch that had as its focal point the queue for a No. 9 bus. Princess Elizabeth joined whole-heartedly in all the by-play, but nevertheless an inherent shyness came across the footlights. Whereas her companion put over her lines with all the

family album by Marcus Adams

Aged four year

Aged nine years

insouciant gaiety of a soubrette destined one day to see her name in lights.

A queue for a No. 9 bus. Of course, I reminded myself, the supporting members of the sketch would know such a queue well enough in real life, but through the accident of their birth the two principals would never have the chance to make friends in such a queue or to experience the communion that such ordinary incidents in everyday existence bring in their train.

I imagine that you would have had the

Delightful Studies by Studio Lisa

same reaction had you been in my seat that afternoon. You would have surely wondered, too, what was to be the future for this high-spirited "starlet", who all through the years of the war had been spending her childhood in complete seclusion in the country. How much freedom would she receive when peace came again? How would she develop as she passed from adolescence to young woman-hood? Most of all, how would she react to the traditional taboos of her background?

*   *   *

The lift had stopped, the footman in the dark-blue battledress and the row of service ribbons on his tunic had opened the gates, and as I came out into the passage, with its long red carpet stretching away into the distance, it was almost as though the question mark was being answered by a small statue in alabaster, placed under a glass cage, and standing on the table now opposite me.

The familiar statue, this time in miniature, of Queen Victoria with her crown firmly planted on her head, her sceptre firmly clasped in her hand, and as firmly seated upon her throne that seemed (even in alabaster) to be as solid as the earth itself.

Would she have approved of her great-great-granddaughter dancing the can-can, even at a private party, just before her nineteenth birthday?

Put like that, the obvious answer one expects would be: "No, she would not have been amused." But in actual fact, had Queen Victoria been present that evening at the American Ambassador's home, in Princes Gate, I am fully convinced that she would have appreciated the performance was so

On the lawn at Royal Lodge

decorous it could have been given at one of the *tableau-vivant* displays that her grandchildren used to get up in her honour each birthday.

For certainly that was the universal impression of all of us who were there that July evening—is it already nearly two years ago? Certainly, having tea at Buckingham Palace with Princess Margaret's lady-in-waiting (on the afternoon I am describing), it was only natural that we should recall that party (and the garbled versions which afterwards appeared in some of the American papers), since Miss Jennifer Bevan had been one of the chorines, too, who took the floor with such success at midnight.

Actually, the cabaret was kept as a great surprise until the last moment. It was a fancy-dress party, and we had all been asked to come as our favourite book or play or tune. Princess Elizabeth and her husband, together with an equerry, were dressed up amusingly to represent *The Waiter, the Porter, and the Upstairs Maid.*

Disguised as an Edwardian parlourmaid, Princess Elizabeth had never looked prettier: in fact, so much prettier than she often appears in her photographs, and, moreover, so much more animated that I found myself recalling a rueful remark made by her younger sister: "The papers *will* turn Lilibet into the 'dull' one and make me 'gay'."

On the terrace at Windsor Castle

When Princess Margaret speaks of her elder sister it is very remarkable to see how her expression changes. At once a kind of glow lights up her face, that special radiance which anyone who has ever been close to the Queen will recognize as being her mother's special prerogative.

Indeed, the devotion of the two sisters for each other is a profound one, only increased by time and separation. As happens in so many other families, the elder sister is now married, the younger one is still at home with the rooms next to her empty, so that she can no longer run in and out of her sister's sitting-room. She herself has as her sanctum at the Palace the high-ceilinged room that was once their shared day-nursery, but with all the childhood objects long since removed.

It is a very grown-up room today, with a study by Vandyck of three horses on one wall, her own desk, littered up with books of reference in a corner by the window, and a heap of current novels and biographies on a table in the centre of the room.

Yet somehow her sanctum, for all its pleasant, lived-in feeling, seems to lack something of the vivid personality of its owner, so that one is constrained to ask whether the Princess does not ever feel lonely in this great house, with its long, echoing corridors and sudden, remote silences.

If the question surprised her, her answer

13

Leaving the Jubilee Service at St. Paul's, 1935

to me was instinctive and immediate. "But this is my home," she said, stressing the last word with the final stamp of truth.

The home, where often on several evenings running the Princess will dine alone with her parents, and sit afterwards with them until bedtime. Sometimes her mother will work on a piece of embroidery, her father struggle at a crossword puzzle, but more often nowadays two of them will play canasta, with the other looking up from his paper to give advice. The rage for this latest transatlantic game has captured the Palace, and there is a set on the table in the Princess' sitting-room.

Before her elder sister was married they shared a passion for charades, any kind of guessing and acting game, and when Princess Margaret is congratulated on her skill at her favourite of all (you divide the company into two sides, and one side goes out of the room, thinks of a long word, and returns a few minutes later to act it, in syllables), the Princess always replies: "It's quite easy if either Lilibet or I are doing it, because there's a kind of telepathy between us."

* * *

I do not know whether the pretty parlour-maid, as she danced round that night at the Douglas' party, with her husband dressed in the tail coat of a waiter and sporting a false

A Younger Sister pays her first visit to have a ride at the Zoo

The Princesses have their first ride on the Underground from St. James's Park to Tottenham Court Road. With them are Lady Helen Graham and "Crawfie"

Charlie Chaplin moustache, had been let into the secret, or guessed on her own, what the cabaret was to be at midnight, but certainly Her Majesty the Queen knew. For she had been consulted by her younger daughter, as she always in consulted about everything, and had given her permission and her blessing.

I am stressing this incident particularly, though it was no more than an incident, because it provides a perfect example of how easy it is for Royalty to be misrepresented, and how difficult it is for any member of the Royal Family ever to make a correction after the event.

No one would deny that the Queen is as wise as any parent in the land as to what her young unmarried daughter should or should not be allowed to do, and on this occasion, when the idea of dressing up had first been mooted by the party's hostess, Miss Sharman Douglas, Princess Margaret had automatically turned to her mother for advice. And Her Majesty's answer had been, "Of course you should do it. It will be great fun for you all."

And it was fun. That is exactly the right word. Harmless and pleasant fun. The lights went down and we sat on cushions on the floor. There was a sudden hush of expectancy, and then through the open doorway, to the familiar strains of the Can-Can music originally associated with the "Folies Bergère", eight pretty girls, one arm round each of their neighbours' shoulders, appeared in a well-drilled line, kicking their legs in perfect time . . . but only to a very modest height and with such a *frou-frou* of petticoats that I wonder they were able to get their feet off the ground at all.

But their gaiety coupled with the music combined to make such a charming effect, and they themselves were so radiantly happy and so young, that the audience went on applauding until a rather breathless encore was given.

Five minutes later Maurice Winnick's band was striking up for us all to take our own partners again, and as I fox-trotted round the room, recalling how it was nearly five years since I had last seen the Princess dance in public, I was struck by a rather interesting comparison. Not in the improvement of her dancing so much as in the improvement of her looks. All her early promise had been fulfilled, as far as her colouring and features were concerned. On the other hand one physical attribute had not changed. Her height.

In fact, that is something which, in a way, strikes one above all else. Today, she possesses the minute perfection of a Dresden figurine. She has the same shiny neatness, the same unruffled self-possession; the same beautifully shaped hands and feet.

Only her mouth seems to belong to someone of larger clay, her eyes to the close-up of a film-star, but for the rest she is exquisitely tiny, and there was one moment that evening at the fancy-dress party which impressed this on my mind for always. It was when the Princess stood in silhouette against a balustrade, talking to her aunt, the Duchess of Kent, who seemed quite to tower over her niece.

Ever since she was a child leaning over the banisters to watch the guests arrive at one of her parents' dinner parties, Princess Margaret has regarded the Duchess of Kent as the best-dressed woman in her own world,

and has secretly been determined to emulate her chic, as she became grown-up herself.

All the same, although since her childhood, too, the Princess has loved to make fashion drawings and designs of the dresses she would wear *one* day, it would be entirely wrong to give the impression that the Princess spends her life today only thinking of the next party, or the next dress she is going to wear.

On the contrary. That afternoon, in the lady-in-waiting's own sitting-room, there was on the desk the typed copy of the speech that the Princess was to deliver the next day at a school for the deaf, near Newbury.

Miss Bevan picked it up and showed it to me, telling me how the draft had been prepared by the Queen's own secretary, and then discussed by the Princess with her lady-in-waiting, who often had to make many alterations before the Princess was satisfied.

And it had distressed the Princess greatly when, not long ago, adverse comments were printed in regard to the text of her speeches, suggesting that they were made of conventional milk-and-water platitudes. "Surely it is the feeling behind them which matters," she protested. "Besides, what do they expect me to do? Stand up and call out, 'Hiya, folks'?"

Those close to the Princess are very conscious of just how much effort she puts into her increasing number of public appearances. How she rehearses her speeches beforehand; goes over them, in the car, right up to the moment of arrival; delivers them with the same brand of irresistible sincerity as her mother and sister; and how, when the ordeal —and it must always be an ordeal for a girl of her age—is over and the return journey home has started, the royal performer always asks, humbly, of her audience, how she has done, and was it truly a success? Not from her own point of view, but from the point of view of the cause she has been trying to aid; and she is so thrilled and reassured when she is able to feel that she really has done something to help. . . .

* * *

How different all people are when one is allowed to see behind the façade. The trouble is, Royalty can never answer back. They are always "news", and unfortunately, if facts are not forthcoming, nonsense is made up, which gains credence by the very reason that tradition forbids members of the Royal Family from making any official denial.

In consequence the Princess exclaimed ruefully to me, "I believe some people

As "Principal Girl" in the Windsor pantomimes

imagine I lie on a sofa all day long waiting for the evening to come and the next party to begin."

In actual fact, most of her mornings are spent going through her considerable correspondence. It is not commonly known—indeed, it was a surprise to myself—that the Princess, like her mother, opens all her letters herself, so there is no need even for her closest friend to write "Personal" at the top of an envelope.

Of course, it is left to her lady-in-waiting to reply to her unknown correspondents, but even then the Princess always indicates exactly what she wants said.

For instance, Miss Bevan, as I came into her room, had been replying to a "fan" from Yorkshire who had succeeded in taking a snapshot of the Princess leaving the village church when staying the week-end with friends. And in her pencilled note across the top of the letter the recipient, after expressing her pleasure in having the snapshot for her private scrapbook, had added: "*Jolly good about her being a nurse, M.*"

How charmingly real and human the scribbled comment was, I was thinking, when the telephone rang on Miss Bevan's desk. It was the Princess speaking from her own apartment at the other end of the long carpeted corridor. But it must be remembered that Royalty does not give interviews—only audiences and in private.

However, later, as I came down in the lift once more to pass the policeman guarding the gates into the open Mall, where girls of the Princess' age were walking hatless and free from their Whitehall offices, I could not help thinking of the answer that she had given when it was suggested that sometimes

she must long to be someone else, just anyone, above all, someone quite different.

To which the King's younger daughter had replied at once and with a conviction in her voice that was like a moving chord in music, "I cannot imagine anything more wonderful than being who I am."

But from the way her expression changed, the sudden look of dedication, it was obvious she was thinking not of herself, but of her family destiny and of her own increasingly important part in its relentless yet rewarding pattern.

AND now let us go back to the beginning and trace this younger sister's progress through the familiar phases of development that stand out like signposts in the lives of all children on their way to maturity.

On the head of every child on the day of its birth I sometimes think the mother sets three crowns. A crown for happiness, a crown for courage, a crown for faith.

Did the mother with the dark hair and the deep blue eyes, lying in a four-poster bed in a room at Glamis Castle, some twenty years ago, have such thoughts about the baby for whom the bells of St. Paul's were ringing out a welcome? Was it the secret hope that she was about to give her husband a son and heir that made her so determined

A Girl Guides' signalling lesson at Windsor Castle, May 30th, 1944

that her second child should be born in her own childhood home?

At least the baby, later to be christened Margaret Rose, had one mark of distinction from the start. Apart from the little girl destined to be Victoria Eugénie of Spain, she was the first member of the Royal Family to be born north of the Border since the arrival of that boy in Dunfermline, in 1600, who was later to wear, in his followers' eyes, a martyr's crown, Charles the First.

Some younger sisters, of course, assume a martyr's crown, but this one was determined at once to stake out her due claims, within the family circle. Indeed, when asked today what is her own first memory, Princess Margaret replies, "I half remember half falling out of my pram. A great to-do. I imagine I must have wanted to be noticed," she adds, with that sudden, disarming smile which is always at the corner of her lips.

Has she a vague recollection, too, of the time when she was taken to her first party, where a conjuror was performing? They tried to make her sit in the front row, but she refused point-blank. "But you'll see so much better," they urged her persuasively. "I shall see too well," the baby princess retorted.

What she cannot possibly remember is that even before she celebrated her first birthday she suddenly started humming the *Merry Widow* waltz. This so astonished her maternal grandmother, Lady Strathmore,

who was holding her at the time, that she almost dropped her charge!

From the very beginning the younger child was precocious and very wide-awake. The Court photographer, summoned to take pictures of the new baby, commented afterwards, "Not once did she whimper or close her eyes. I was very struck by the quick way she seemed to take notice, for so young a child."

On her third birthday, celebrated at Glamis, Sir James Barrie came over to tea. His small hostess was sitting entranced, staring at one of her presents, a little toy table, with two painted flower-pots on it, the whole thing about the size of a thimble, whereupon the author of *Peter Pan* asked her, "Is that really yours?" To which she replied at once, "It is mine *and* yours."

Duet in harmony

The Princess makes her first speech at the age of thirteen

The portrait of the Princess in Sea Ranger's uniform was taken by Dorothy Wilding

This answer so intrigued the famous dramatist that he incorporated it in the text of his play *The Boy David*. He also made due acknowledgment of its source by promising its creator a penny royalty for every time that particular line was spoken on the stage. Four years later, when Barrie lay dying in a nursing-home, he sent his secretary, Lady Cynthia Asquith, with a bag of pennies to the Princess' London home, and in return received a contract solemnly signed by the child and witnessed by her mother.

Doubtless the little girl was glad enough to have this sudden windfall, for unlike her sister, who received a shilling a week pocket money, Margaret had to rely usually on the generosity of Alah, who occasionally, in the omnipotent way of nannies, would produce half-a-crown, which was expected to last a very long time!

Now you could not find a more devoted example of that, alas, dying-out hierarchy than Alah, who having already lost her elder charge to a governess, tried to keep her baby to herself as long as possible in the nurseries, high up under the glass dome at No. 145, Piccadilly.

However, the moment Alah's back was turned the infant would escape down the three flights of stairs, peep round the dining-room door, and time her arrival cunningly to coincide with the coffee stage. Squeezing against her father's knee, she would get her reward of a tiny fistful of special sugar crystals.

It was easy to see that her father adored her—perhaps perversely because she was not the hoped-for boy. Anyway, he has admitted many times since that Lilibet's sister could persuade the pearl to come out of any oyster. Even today he can refuse her nothing; and

though a man of considerable reserve himself, he may sometimes have been made shy by the way that his younger daughter would fling her arms round his neck and cover his cheeks with kisses; yet secretly he was warmed by her excess of affection for Papa.

Today she pronounces his name as if both the "a's" were short, almost in the French style, like this—Păpă—while Mummie is still Mummie when the Princess is talking to her personal circle of friends, though the family no longer indulge in the uproarious games of racing demon, or fierce pillow fights that were each evening bedtime's prelude at No. 145, Piccadilly.

How desperately anxious the parents were that the accident of royal birth should not be a constricting handicap to their children, but that they should be brought up as simply and unselfconsciously as possible. They themselves, at that time, infinitely preferred to dine together alone in the evenings, and in the same way the children entertained their contemporaries very seldom to tea parties, but lived in a little world of their own, grooming the thirty toy horses that stood in a semi-circle on the top landing under the glass dome, and playing their own versions of touch and rig, in Hamilton Gardens at the back of their home, bordering on Hyde Park. Often their father would join them there, and using a convenient statue of Byron as home, would show a fine turn of speed in outwitting his would-be captors.

While, through the railings, the public stared at the two little girls, always bare-headed, in their sensible tweed skirts and woolly jerseys. "Didn't you find all those staring faces an embarrassment?" someone asked Princess Margaret. Whereupon she shook her head. "It's strange, you know," she answered, "but somehow, right from the beginning, I don't seem to remember noticing. . . ."

But they must have noticed (the crowds surging forward cutting short the expedition) the day that, greatly daring, they made their one and only sortie into the normal life outside their London front door. A trip by Underground, and for their destination the Y.W.C.A., Tottenham Court Road. You can imagine their excitement before the event, when you appreciate that hitherto to watch the Aberdeen fish express

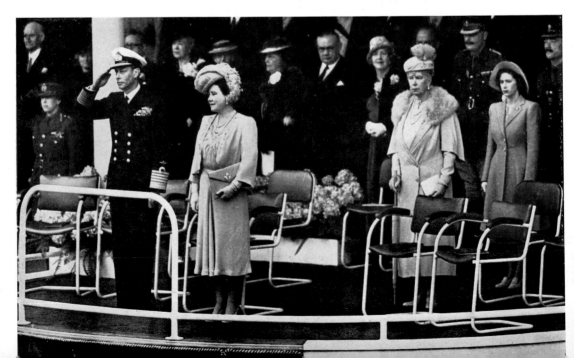

1

ROYAL OCCASIONS

1. *The King takes the salute at the Victory Parade*
2. *At Buckingham Palace, on the balcony, after the Coronation, 1937*
3. *Wimbledon finals watched by the Royal Family, July 4th, 1947*
4. *V.E. Day, 1945*

2

3

4

race through Glamis station had been the highlight of their holidays in Scotland. Especially when they discovered chewing-gum in the station slot-machine and stretched it between the rails to see what would happen when the wheels of the train went over it.

Was there chewing-gum in their coat pockets the day they sallied forth with the Duchess' lady-in-waiting, Lady Helen Graham, as their chaperone to the party? It is on record that, much to her delight, Margaret was allowed to pay her own fare out of her own purse, while again at the Y.W.C.A. they purchased their own tea, collecting their tray standing in the queue and choosing just what they wanted. . . .

"Margaret always wants what I want." How many other elder sisters have made a similar protest, and heard echoing in their ears the eternal shrill plaint dogging their every footstep of "Wait for me, wait for me." Lilibet seems to have been extraordinarily patient, but even so she possessed a temper that could flare up suddenly, while Margaret in one of her moods could be as exasperating as any other junior member of a family.

Then there would be a sudden storm, with such lung-power used that it is strange now, looking back, that there should ever have been a moment when a persistent rumour spread through the country that Margaret had been born dumb.

Dumb. It is the very last adjective that one would ever use to describe the childhood life of that plump little figure who enjoyed nothing more than a good "scene", and when her undoubted charm and dramatic flair failed to extricate herself from the results of her temperament, was not averse to engaging in a display of fisticuffs. Inevitably getting the worst of all-in fighting with her adversary, four years her senior, she would end up by biting, and biting hard.

It was little use reprimanding her, or threatening that she would not hear her favourite story at bedtime, *The Little Red Hen*. The child had the gift of the easy answer that turneth away wrath. "Oh, Crawfie, laugh, *laugh* . . ." she would say to her beloved governess, who so often eventually had to oblige. . . . While on another occasion, when she was receiving a rather pompous lecture for some misdemeanour, she entirely broke up the atmosphere by opening her eyes very wide and singing, *Who's afraid of the Big Bad Wolf?*

On yet another occasion, when she was four years old, the little Princess was found under the luncheon table, much to the surprise of her parents' grown-up guests. The only reason why she was discovered was that, bored with the endless prattle of the grown-ups, she had started to tickle one or two of the more inviting ankles that she could see.

Then there were her dreams. The most fantastic surrealist dreams. Margaret would start recounting them at breakfast, and without drawing breath, continue from climax to climax, in the vain hope of staving off lessons. How true the substance of these dreams was she can't be sure—even today—at what point her imagination took over, for right from the very beginning she possessed the real storyteller's technique of complete self-deception. Added to which she had the timing skill of the born comedienne, and had already found a rather unexpected ally in her paternal grandfather, although

At the Royal Windsor Horse Show

she confesses now, looking back, that she was terrified of him as a small girl.

All the same, at one period in her childhood, she had a pact with King George V that at 10.30 a.m. precisely she would wave her handkerchief out of the window on the promise that he would do the same from his study at Buckingham Palace. After his death, she was heard to remark, "Grandpapa is in Heaven now, and I am sure God finds him very useful."

Incidentally, contrary to legend, the Princess never referred to him as "Grandpapa *England*". "I never called him that, ever," she says most emphatically today.

In a way the King's passing hardly touched her. She was not allowed to go to his funeral, she was too small. Rather it was her Uncle David's disappearance from the scene that upset her more . . . for he had given them all the A. A. Milne books, *Winnie the Pooh* and *When We Were Very Young*, of which Margaret's own favourite

was, not surprisingly, *Changing the Guard at Buckingham Palace*.

That was about the greatest day-to-day excitement in the children's lives, plus, as a great treat, annual visits to a pantomime and the horse show at Olympia. For the rest, Lilibet and Margaret were perfectly happy and content to play at week-ends at Royal Lodge, in and out of their very own house, with its name on the gate, "Bwthyn Bach".

The Little Thatched House. Presented to Princess Elizabeth by the Welsh people, and exquisitely complete, even to an oil painting to scale of their mother, hung over the drawing-room mantelpiece. Here they could cook and scrub, and pour out tea, playing the game that is a favourite of all children, the game of pretending to be grown up.

And then, one afternoon, they came in to grown-up tea in the drawing-room, to find that their adored Uncle David had brought his week-end guests over from Fort Belvedere. Now future events were beginning to cast their shadow across that happily self-

A canter on the sands during the South African tour

contained and private household. Until the afternoon came when the announcement of the Abdication was made in the House of Commons, and on the top floor of their London home the two sisters stood, hand in hand, their noses pressed against the glass, staring down wonderingly at the great concourse gathered in the streets.

The news was broken to them by explaining that from now on they would be going to live in Buckingham Palace. "*What! For always?*" echoed Lilibet, in horrified tones. Her younger sister's reaction was slightly different. "Bother!" she said. "Just when I had learnt to write 'Margaret Rose of York'." Into the silence she added plaintively, "Now that Papa has turned King, I am nothing." A moment later she was dragging her sister back to the nursery for a game of racing demon.

But she couldn't stop the clock, either, racing on to her bedtime, or the future. That phase of her childhood was over, for ever.

Three

FOR no one does Life divide itself easily into neat compartments. So many years exactly for growth, so many for education, so many for family dependence. The different phases in a human being's evolution towards maturity have a habit of overlapping, the external details especially of repeating themselves, until one finds oneself exclaiming, "Why, this is where we came in . . . this is the exact spot where I stood once before . . . is it already ten years ago?"

The next instant, the present has captured all one's attention again. All the same, perhaps for an instant, Princess Elizabeth's chief bridesmaid, as she advanced down the nave of Westminster Abbey, so slim and graceful in her flowing net dress, had a fleeting vision of that plump little pudding of a girl, who ten years before had walked just as slowly, with just as many eyes upon her, until at one moment she had tripped and almost fallen over her diminutive train.

"I want it to be as *long* as Lilibet's," she had pleaded and wailed on that occasion. Nevertheless, for her father's Coronation it remained just that much shorter, and other younger sisters will sympathize.

However, she was delighted with the special lightweight coronet that her father had had designed for her to wear with her royal cloak edged with ermine at his crowning: so delighted that Margaret would appear at tea sometimes—"I'm wearing it to practise"—and swagger up and down, carrying a walking-stick. "What are you pretending to be *now*?" her mother would ask, patiently taking her cue. "Why, can't you guess? I'm Johnnie Walker."

It was hardly the answer one would expect from a child, so inexorably shut away from the outside world, but then this was an unexpected child, in every way, as the years ahead were to prove. One who was determined to copy her elder sister in everything, and yet was so utterly unlike her in character.

For Lilibet not only had a passion for neatness, which was almost a mania, whereas Margaret at that time was a complete tomboy, but Lilibet also had inherited the shyness, almost bordering on acute self-consciousness sometimes, of her father, and her aunt, the Princess Royal, while Margaret would not have known what the word "inhibition" meant, even if it had been explained to her.

Further, Princess Elizabeth could never show affection easily, would only love a very few people in her whole life, but these fortunate few with such an absolute devotion that her feeling became like a sacrament.

Whereas Margaret fell in and out of love every day of her childhood with something, someone. And equally, fell in and out of trouble, too, though there are many apocryphal stories told of her childhood which the Princess now denies with some emphasis as having no basis in fact. Such as the picturesque tale that she once pulled the plug out of the bottom of the boat when she was having a rowing lesson on the lake in Windsor Park.

"I just wanted to see what would happen," she has been quoted as saying afterwards, but when I read that her companion on that occasion was a Girl Guide mistress, I could not help feeling that the anecdote had a false ring about it, which was fully confirmed by the Princess' own comment that had an air of finality about it. "One isn't able to do things like that," she said. "If one is dressed in a Girl Guide or Sea Ranger uniform and rowing a boat with others in it, one would not only have a responsibility to them, one would be under orders."

All the same the young Princess, so full of healthy spirits, so unconquerably buoyant, could have been the female version of the *Punch* joke about the harassed mother instructing her elder offspring to go in search of his younger brother. "And when you find him, see what he's a-doing of, and tell him to stop it at once. . . ."

The phraseology and background might be different, but the nervous need for constant supervision remained the same. There

Growing up with the telephone

Presenting the prizes at St. Edmund's School, Canterbury

Meeting one of the prizes at a new housing estate

was, for instance, the first occasion when the two children made an appearance at one of their parents' garden parties at Buckingham Palace. "Margaret, if you see someone wearing a funny hat, you are *not* to point," her senior by four lofty years admonished her. "Why not? Because . . ."

But Margaret was already pulling the elastic that tied their own hats sharply under the chin, dissolving the argument into triumphant if painful action. Anyway, what was allowed and what wasn't? It is the question mark that confronts every growing child, the barbed-wire fence that separates a boy or girl from the comparative independence of adolescence. In this case, apart altogether from the restrictive barriers of their birth, there was soon to be another complication. The war.

In 1940, after Dunkirk, with invasion threatening, many counsellors urged the King to send his daughters, the two nearest heirs to his throne, to safety overseas. He refused. Or, rather, their mother said most positively, "I would not let them go without me, and I cannot leave the King."

I remember thinking that nevertheless it could not have been an easy choice . . . the afternoon that later in the war I found myself in a sitting-room on the first floor of Buckingham Palace. There were two arm-chairs, a writing desk, an electric fire, and most of the windows were boarded up with cardboard. My lasting impression, looking back now, was that it was a very small room.

Directly below in the forecourt the bomb had fallen, but although the world soon saw the pictures of the damage, it was a well-kept secret that the King and Queen had not been in the shelter at the time, but in

Princess Margaret in her St. John's uniform

C

that sitting-room which they used whenever they could be alone together throughout the war years.

"We all rushed out from our own rooms when the crash came," the Queen's lady-in-waiting, Lady Delia Peel, told me, "and immensely to our relief, the door opened and the Queen came out, followed by the King. 'I think we had better go below now,' Her Majesty said, and they walked down the stairs as unconcernedly as though they were about to hold a Court."

No one outside knew what a narrow escape they had had. An hour later, when the all clear went, they immediately drove out to visit the East End, and the Queen sympathizing with the bombed-out victims there said quietly, "Our home has been hit, too." But how thankful she must have been at that moment to know that her children were in a comparatively safe place.

When you come to think of it, it is quite a surprise to realize now that from the age of nearly ten to rising fifteen Margaret was closeted there at Windsor. When she disappeared from public sight she was still a little football—her own description later—when she came out on VE Day, mingling for the first and only time in her life with the crowd and knocking off a few hats happily to celebrate her momentary freedom, she was a teenager, rid of her puppy fat, and with already an air of sophistication far beyond her years, that was to make her appear almost to be her sister's contemporary.

This was due partly to the impulses of her nature, partly to environment and the influences of those five years. Through the impingement of war, she found herself more and more in the company of men. True,

she and her sister both went on with their Girl Guide activities, but these sorties in the Park were intended more to give her self-discipline and self-reliance than to serve as a form of social activity. True again, she got on extremely well with her fellow Guiders, and there were always shrieks of laughter coming from under the canvas of the tent where the younger Princess was camping out. But she was equally at ease with the young Guards officers who were on duty inside the Castle.

They would take it in turn to have the privilege of lunching with the Princesses, who would find their conversation a welcome change from lessons—"Thank goodness," Princess Margaret remarked to me reflectively, "whenever my German lesson started the sirens seemed to go and I used to escape"—yes, but it was another kind of escape down to the lunch-table. One of their guests, a young Grenadier officer at the time, spoke to me the other day of his impressions of his two hostesses.

"If you sat at Princess Margaret's end of the table," he said, "the conversation never lapsed for a moment. You did not have to worry at all yourself. She was amazingly self-assured without being embarrassingly so. In fact, looking back now, it's extraordinary what a good companion she already was. You did not think of her as being any particular age . . . and certainly there couldn't have been anyone less like a sub-deb at a dance."

She was certain herself that she was quite old enough to go to dances! At least, she protested so vehemently to her parents that she was, that they used to find themselves giving way whenever there was a small party for troops in the neighbourhood.

It was only at week-ends that the King and Queen came down to Windsor themselves and the Royal Standard would fly for a short time over the Castle. They would both be desperately tired, the King with masses of State papers to attend to, and Ministers to see, the Queen longing to be quiet and domesticated with her children. But at the same time both were determined that young men, who might be going overseas at any moment and had been deprived through their Service training of peace-time happiness and gaiety, should have at least something to remember.

That something might turn out to be afternoon invitations like the ones for Canadian airmen when Princess Margaret and Princess Elizabeth would slowly disappear from view, completely surrounded by kind and smiling faces. Or it might take the form of an informal supper, when after-

wards they would turn back the rugs and dance to the gramophone and Margaret would sip champagne when her mother wasn't looking, and still be on the improvised dance floor at midnight.

That did not happen every week-end by any means, though once, when Philip Mountbatten and David Milford Haven appeared on leave together, the two sisters danced happily, making a foursome, for three nights running. In fact, just because the parties were such impromptu affairs, it was difficult to refuse her permission to stay up.

Thus the taste, not for champagne, but for dancing with pleasant and handsome young men in uniform, was fed by chance propinquity, while they, in their turn, forgetting that she was still a child, talked to her of the shows they had seen on leave in London, the singers they had enjoyed in night clubs, the social gossip they had heard of the world she would one day inhabit.

So it was not surprising that one day when her sister was at Eton studying constitutional history with the Provost, Sir Henry Marten, Margaret sat in her room copying out an imaginary letter that could be regarded as a lesson in social etiquette. Anyway, this was the letter, from first to last entirely her own composition.

Dear Lady Godiva, I am so thrilled with your invitation to your dance, which sounds such fun. I shall do my very best to bring a partner, and would Lord Tulip do? Wasn't it wonderful fun at the meet on Monday? I did think Lady Adcock overdid it a bit with that hat of hers at church, didn't you? Thank you again so much, Yours affectionately, Diaphenia.

The mocking signature was well-chosen, because diaphanous still were her dreams of the day when, no longer a schoolgirl, she would be able to enjoy some of the ordinary pleasures, such as theatre-going, that she had only heard of second-hand in snatches during those five years long at Windsor.

Yet even later, when she was nearly seventeen, it still remained a tremendous treat for her to lunch in a public restaurant. In fact, she did so for the first time as the guest of her father's cousin, Queen Ena of Spain, who sent a message over the telephone to ask whether her guest would rather lunch upstairs privately in her apartment, or downstairs in the ordinary dining-room. . . .

Promptly came back the reply, "Downstairs, please, so that I can see the people. . . ."

The people . . . that would always be her instinctive response, even as it was on that afternoon after Princess Elizabeth's wedding, when the sister-left-behind came up to their floor of the Palace, and looked down from the windows of their old nursery at the crowds packing the Mall, cheering the bridal car disappearing towards Waterloo.

Only a few minutes before, Princess Margaret had been down there herself at the gates, scattering paper rose leaves over the newly married couple. Now, still in her bridesmaid's dress, she stood quite alone at the window, thinking perhaps of VE night, when just for once she had been allowed to mingle with the outside world, thinking right back over the ten years from the Coronation of their father to the end of this chapter, that also had had its setting inside the Abbey. (It was an end as well as a beginning.) *I want to be like Lilibet, I want to be like Lilibet.* . . .

For didn't that figure at the window, that

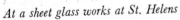

At a sheet glass works at St. Helens

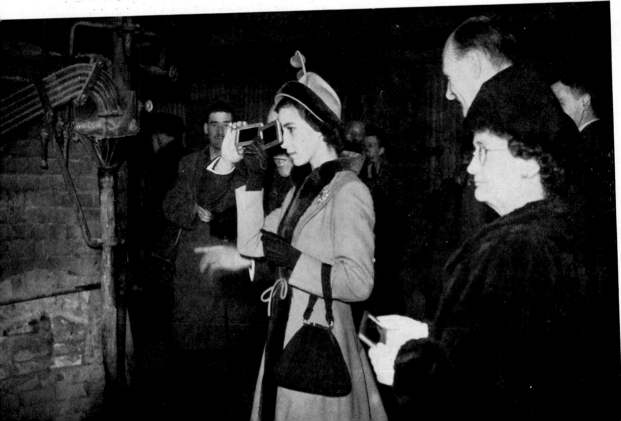

Christening group for Prince Charles

figure who had so recently burgeoned into beauty, remember too (as we all remember echoes of our childhood selves) the perpetual parrot cry of the little girl she had been herself ten years ago? If she did, it must also have come to her with a glowing stab of awareness that from now on she would be copying no one. No one.

Instead, she would be taking her own appointed place in the dedicated pattern that had made her whole family so infinitely beloved.

Already, of course, the Princess had had a taste of the inexorable discipline of that pattern, when she had recently accompanied her parents to South Africa. There would be many more such royal tours ahead, many to make henceforth on her own. How would she manage? How would she compare?

That question mark was more than a challenge; it was a summons to be answered with loyal and dutiful pride in the years of growing maturity ahead.

All the same, it wouldn't always be easy.

Princess Margaret has received many gifts, but none that gave her more pleasure than the strawberry which six-year-old Roger Williams had grown in his garden at the East Grinstead Home for Blind Children

Four

FROM the day of their birth the heirs-apparent to the British throne have a position, rigidly defined, rigidly observed. For a younger sister, however close to that throne, as Princess Margaret is, her official duties have no exact complement. This means that the amount of public work she accepts is her own personal prerogative.

Actually, Princess Margaret was not yet fourteen when she made her first speech in public, during a visit to the school named after herself, in Windsor. On that occasion, wearing a pink cotton dress with short white sleeves, she received purses from twenty-five of the pupils, past and present, in aid of a rebuilding fund. A simple, modest ceremony to be duplicated later on, many times over, and always on a substantially larger scale. Nevertheless, the visit to the Margaret Rose School had considerable significance, for it meant that the first milestone in her career as a royal servant of the public was successfully passed.

There is a picture of the young Princess taken that July afternoon in 1944, with her mother looking on, ready to prompt her, if necessary. It wasn't, then, or now. All the same, it must have been a considerable ordeal, and even today, after having made dozens of much more testing public appearances, the Princess confesses she still has the equivalent of "first night nerves" every time

With her elder sister at the British Legion poppy factory at Richmond

Princess Margaret opens a Youth Week at Bethnal Green

that she drives on her way to fulfil a date in her increasingly packed diary.

"But after all those performances in pantomime?" I echoed. "Didn't that make it easier to face *any* audience?" The Princess only shakes her head emphatically at the suggestion. *That* was simply fun, make believe; professional perfection was neither expected nor sought; *this* is something so very different, the serious, dedicated side of her life, the return in service for all that has been given her. And it is good that she should be openly conscious

World Conference of Girl Guides at Oxford

of that debt, good that she should say in that musical voice that contains so many echoes of her mother's, "I always feel so very anxious not to disappoint anyone who

Annual tea party of the "Not Forgotten" Association

has come to see me, and perhaps waited a long time."

However, no trace of the nerves which can harry her show either in her face or delivery in public. On the contrary, she seems most beautifully self-possessed, putting at ease everyone round her, as she moves punctually through the time-table of each programme, unflagging, whatever its length, with the grace of her youth, but the dignity of someone of her mother's generation. Moreover,

At the Brady Girls' Club, Stepney

gaps in the trees at the lower side, while at the top of the wide, untrammelled field, above the serried tiers of excited youngsters, a sea of dark blue uniforms, ten thousand of them all told, was the bright line of the delegates' banners, a brilliant splash of colour against the coming dusk.

Slowly, as a final preparation for the Princess' arrival, the delegates from all over the world made their way to marching music towards the centre of the field, where

The Princess signs at Toynbee Hall

I write that after having watched her most important public appearances last summer with deliberately critical eyes.

The venue was the "Camp Fire" of the 13th World Conference of Girl Guides, held on Headington Hill, just outside Oxford, almost exactly six years after her first public appearance. On this present occasion the King's second daughter was on show and on duty for over four hours, but happily it was one of those summer evenings which, when they do flower, make one conscious that there is no more beautiful country in the world than Britain.

Indeed, it would scarcely have been possible not to have been stirred by the scene on that green hillside outside Oxford, with the college towers silhouetted through the a space had been preserved and a small platform erected, with microphones laid on that would at the right moment transcribe the message of the Sea Rangers' Commodore across the seven seas. But first she must accept the scrolls, twenty-seven of them, with the messages of friendship within, from the hands of chosen Guiders, and pass them on, each to a different country, Shropshire to Mexico, Gloucestershire to the Philippines, the Isle of Man to Guatemala. . . .

The delegates, with their variegated skins and uniforms and their variegated attempts at making a royal curtsey, had their moment alone in the centre of the arena—"this scroll has been passed from hand to hand down the Pilgrims' Way and now goes to Brazil" —and then disappeared again into the anonymous host. But surely that moment would stay in their memory, recounted to their countrywomen for a long time; and the impact of that moment, too, when before the sing-song and the lighting of the camp fire, in the now quickening dusk, the Princess paused at the last paragraph of her speech and then added, in a firm evocative voice:

"We shall always be loyal to our ideals, which never change with time or custom; and we believe that, by our example, we shall help to establish a true and lasting friendship among the nations of the world."

Trite platitudes? Empty truisms? It is easy enough to read thus, with a cynical curl of the lips, not so easy, had you been there, as I was, and heard the stillness of the great audience and the warmth in the speaker's voice that was being carried, by the miracle of radio, to the ends of the earth.

Indeed, as I slipped away between the gap in the trees, I found myself wishing that all those—and it would be foolish to pretend there are not a minority—who visualize Princess Elizabeth's sister merely as a pretty clothes peg on which to hang a succession of the latest fashions had been there that evening, too.

For I think the critics might have changed their mind. Certainly they could hardly have failed to be impressed by the manner in which the chief guest at the camp fire had worn her dark blue uniform, with the plain serviceable beret, and had progressed slowly right across the arena, now saluting, now smiling to acknowledge the wave after wave of applause from her fellow Guiders.

With the regulation flat heels to her Service shoes, she looked tinier than ever, but that seemed an asset on this occasion, since this was an evening of celebration, taken over by youth. And now that her sister is a mother for the second time, it is as the representative and spokesman of youth that Princess Margaret is eager to assume increasing responsibility.

That sense of responsibility, not to be just a stuffed dummy but a real human being, fulfilling a useful purpose, made her, when still in her teens, announce to the group of officials round her, "I don't very much care for the name of our League." It was the Scottish Children's League of Pity, of which the Princess is honorary President. Has the title, I wonder, now been changed?

The Princess has also inherited from her grandmother, Queen Mary, a very human curiosity for poking in corners, and not being content simply to observe the outward show; it is what goes on behind the elaborate

Bridesmaid at St. Margaret's, Westminster

"spit-and-polish" of a royal visit that intrigues her most, and can sometimes give colour to what might otherwise have been a dullish ceremony.

And should there be an unexpected contretemps, she enjoys that most of all! For example, there was the occasion when she and her sister were the guests of the evening at a charity ball. After they had been ceremoniously conducted to the top of the stairs leading to the ballroom, the key of the special door could not be found, and there they were. "What fun," exclaimed the younger Princess audibly, "something has gone wrong."

Then there was that moment during the South African tour when the wife of a local councillor curtseyed so slowly and so deeply to the Princess' parents that she got stuck and was unable, for some seconds, to get off the ground again. Whereupon Princess Margaret noticeably had the greatest difficulty not to burst out laughing.

However, the Princess is no longer a teenager, and her progress in the extremely complicated art of public life is shown by the reference made at the reopening of the L.C.C. Training College by the Minister of Education. "I have recently heard many speeches at the openings of schools and colleges," Mr. Tomlinson declared, "but Her Royal Highness' was the best."

Here is one sentence of what the Princess herself said. "Your career is second to none of the careers open to women." As she spoke those words, perhaps, she had a passing thought for her own career, which from now on is likely to be extremely exhausting in "term time". And I have sometimes wondered—haven't you?—how far ahead official

engagements are planned and accepted by members of the Royal Family. Again, how many are spaced over a month? Is there a limit to the number of Presidencies, patronages, etc., assumed by any one member of the family? Above all, who finally cries, "Enough"?

Well, in Princess Margaret's case, it is her mother, not her father, who acts as her unofficial comptroller. Since her marriage, Princess Elizabeth has had her own comptroller, General Browning, and her own secretary, but at the moment of writing Princess Margaret's entire entourage consists of one lady-in-waiting, Miss Jennifer Bevan, a girl very little older than herself, who has had to learn as she went along, since inevitably she was as new to all the paraphernalia of royal tours as her employer.

In fact, rather more so, though Miss Bevan had served a short apprenticeship as a member of the household of the present Canadian Governor-General, Lord Alexander. On her return to England she was chosen by the Queen not simply for her attractive appearance—she is a brunette with small delicate features—nor for the suitability of her family background, but for a reason that might have escaped some people. Miss Bevan was not a personal friend of the Princess or a member of the Palace's younger set. Obviously, it might have created difficulties if she had been, at the beginning. As things have turned out, their working relationship has developed into one of friendship through all the experiences they have shared together.

For by the end of the day's programme they certainly both have had to perform

their quota, the one girl who has had to do all the shaking of hands, the other who has had to walk always three yards behind and keep a weather eye open to smooth over any hiatus. There is also all the desk work, too, that Miss Bevan has to get through, the letters to answer, the timetables to check down to the last second, which cannot always be an easy matter, since in one week alone last summer, between May 15th and May 22nd, Princess Margaret made no less than six public appearances, ranging from an Empire Youth Sunday service in Westminster Abbey to a gala performance at Sadler's Wells.

Yes, but the Princess wasn't at the theatre as a private member of the audience, to sit back at leisure and enjoy the performance, she was there to do a "job"—part of the same job that has already made her the honorary Colonel-in-Chief of the Highland Light Infantry (and of the Highland Light Infantry of Canada, too), the President of Dr. Barnardo's Homes, the Commandant-in-Chief of the Nursing Cadets of the St. John's Ambulance Brigade, and Patron of more than half a dozen institutions, like the Scottish Association of Girls' Clubs, the English Folk Dance and Song Society, and the National Pony Society.

There are already many more, of course, and clearly a multitude still to come. Meanwhile, every invitation, whether it arrives at the Palace in a straightforward official envelope, or comes first, unofficially, by word of mouth through a personal friend, is studied impersonally on its merits. Yet even though its merits may be great and the cause deserving of royal patronage, it cannot hope to reach the top of the pile unless it is particularly suitable for someone of Princess Margaret's age and natural sympathies.

That is the final test, while this is the procedure. The Queen's own secretary, Major Harvey, shows each new batch of requests to the Princess' mother, who studies them, marks some of them, and then consults her daughter. Always the Princess makes the final decision herself. For example, when recently she became the new President of the Sunshine Home for Blind Babies, that was entirely her own wish, in fact, almost her own idea. Moreover, the moment that she had accepted the Presidency, she asked to be invited to visit one of the Homes, and as a memento of that occasion one cannot help remembering the snapshot taken of the Princess with a strawberry given her by a little blind boy, who had grown it in the garden of that East Grinstead Branch.

The picture was infinitely touching, but it wasn't touched up. It just happened, a spontaneous incident during her visit, just as it was equally felicitous, the gesture which made her, when she was launching her first ship, *The Edinburgh Castle*, in Belfast, take a rose from her bouquet and place it in the buttonhole of the mechanic who had been chosen to present the flowers.

No doubt he will always remember that second in his life, but I do not doubt also that a far greater impression was left on the Princess by the look of shy delight on his face than by the fact that she was the last person to be made a member of the Imperial Order of the Crown of India. She and her sister received it together, but its heritage belongs to the past, their royal destiny to the future.

*The Archbishop and the Dean of Canterbury show their Royal
guest round the precincts of the Cathedral*

Now I have heard it suggested that Princess Margaret, with her zest for enjoying life, does not give herself up as much to public duties as did her sister at the same age. So I decided I would check up on that, and I discovered that, in actual fact, at the present time the younger sister has as heavy a list of engagements as Princess Elizabeth had at any moment before her marriage.

I was shown the official engagement book laid out on the lady-in-waiting's desk in Buckingham Palace. Page after page pencilled in with official duties. As Miss Bevan put away the book, remarking how the Princess can look up and see exactly what she will be doing three months ahead, and sometimes even six, she added:

"Of course, it will be much harder going from now on, but I cannot imagine that anyone could be more considerate to work for. I have never seen the Princess lose either her temper or her sense of humour. She never gives orders to any member of the household, but always says, 'Please, would you mind . . . ?' "

Then the girl with the plain dark blue dress and unobtrusive prettiness got up from her desk. She was finished for the day, at liberty to go home. We could both see the Princess' car disappearing through the Palace gates, for she was on her way to an informal cocktail party at the home of the young Duchess of Northumberland. So for the rest of the evening the Princess, too, was free. . . .

How free? Well, for a few hours free from any fixed timetable. But how really free is her private life? It is a considerable question mark, which I will try to answer in the next chapter.

Princess Margaret meets the star of "ITMA"

Five

I HAVE often recalled a conversation I had with Margaret Truman when I was her family's guest at the White House. She was showing me the long drawing-room where the diplomatic receptions are held, and where she practises for many hours each day alone at her singing. And while she sat at the grand piano she talked to me very frankly of the complications of being the President's daughter.

The Princess with a Prime Minister

Not simply from the point of view of her career as a singer, the feeling that she sometimes played to packed theatres merely because of the public curiosity to see a Truman perform. But also of the problems of her private life, of having a private life at all.

"If I happen to go out two nights in the same week with the same escort, half the columnists have us engaged at once, which is mighty embarrassing for me"—she confessed ruefully—"but even more so for the young man in the picture. Why, he sometimes becomes too scared even to ring me up again!" Whereupon my hostess in that great gold room shut down the piano lid with a bang and added feelingly, "I guess it must be just as bad, if not worse, these days, for your Princess Margaret. . . ."

I guess it must be, too . . . except that I suppose there is a certain safety in numbers, and a certain wry amusement for the Princess in wondering who will be the next victim suddenly picked out and spotlighted from among her personal circle of friends.

At least, no British paper has committed the *gaffe* of that American magazine which, in publishing their own "inside" list of prospective suitors and eligible grooms, included the name of Lord Derby . . . who had already gone to the altar with another bride!

However, that miss was hardly wider of the mark than the confident prediction of one of our own papers, already two summers ago now, that because the Duke of Marlborough's heir had been invited, together with his sister, to stay at Balmoral, he was ardently courting his host's younger daughter.

However, the only evidence that could be

The Princess with a film star

produced of this "romance" was that on one occasion this young officer in the Life Guards, marching at the head of a troop of men past Buckingham Palace, gave the eyes right as they passed under the Princess' window. No doubt to lessen the monotony and boredom of drill routine.

No one who knows Sunny Blandford could help liking him for his conspicuously good manners, his unfailingly cheerful demeanour, and his eagerness to please; but equally any friend of the family would agree at the unlikeliness of linking his name with that

of the Princess, except as another member of her own set of friends. Moreover, it would be true to say that Lord Blandford is quite as much a member of that set because his sister, Lady Rosemary Spencer Churchill, is among the Princess' half-dozen closest girl friends.

As the Princess herself remarks a little wistfully sometimes, "The papers seldom dwell on my girl friends, like Caroline, Rachel and Laura. Actually, I spend far more time in their company than with anyone else."

Rachel is Rachel Brand, who lives with her family in a block of flats off the Edgware Road, and, refusing to be just another pretty debutante, has volunteered to work in a hospital and likes it; Caroline is a niece of the Duchess of Gloucester, and the sister of Lord Dalkeith, of whom more in a moment, while Laura is Laura Smith, the eldest daughter of Lady Hambledon, who is tall and magnificent in appearance, and has been one of the Queen's ladies-in-waiting.

So it was only natural that the two girls, who are contemporaries, should become friends. Laura Smith has had a considerable success ever since she "came out", though her looks lack the quality of her mother's beauty. But she possesses a lively intelligence, is able to keep up with the quicksilver swiftness of Princess Margaret's own mind, and shares with the other two members of the triumvirate one feature in common. She has very striking eyes.

All the same, were they all four to take part in an "eyes competition", anonymous and unknown, the royal entrant would undoubtedly carry off the prize, for her eyes are truly most remarkable; in fact, a great deal more remarkable than any photograph has yet been able to suggest.

So much so that it is quite a surprise to discover, close to, their extreme lustre, a very intense shade of deep blue. Which, so far as I was concerned, gave new point to the story of the Princess commanding one of her favourite partners, one night at the 400 Club: "Look closely into my eyes. Didn't you realize before that you are actually gazing into the most beautiful eyes in England?"

After the Garter Ceremony at Windsor Princess Margaret, in company with the Duchess of Kent, Princess Olga, and the Duchess of Gloucester, on the steps of St. George's Chapel

This was the Princess' way of mocking an unexpected claim that had recently been made on her behalf in yet another American paper. And it is this brand of mocking humour, so sharply defined in her make-up —even her voice in private life has a slightly mocking lilt to the middle of each sentence —which makes it so much easier for those round her to be at complete ease in her company, though one of the young men on the list of "possibles" confessed to me the other day, "If only she wasn't who she is,

Her family scrapbook contains many pictures of the aunt whose elegance and beauty set her a standard from childhood

Two shipyard apprentices share the great moment of their life

I would propose to her tomorrow! She has by far the most attractive personality of any girl I know."

Yes, but how can one tell that if he had proposed, and the object of his admiration had not been who she always will be, that she would have accepted him?

I think the only person who might come near answering that question and all the others bordering on the same theme—and it is only natural that the world should be curious—would be the Duke of Buccleuch's daughter, Caroline, who is, perhaps, the closest of all the Princess' girl friends; certainly much closer than Sharman Douglas, though the friendship between the ex-

American Ambassador's daughter and the younger daughter of the King of England has been much publicized.

So much so that many people have commented with surprise that the two girls should apparently have such a great deal in common. As a matter of fact, I have a shrewd feeling that the basis of their friendship is one that can often prove a very strong bond: the attraction of opposites.

Sharman is the daughter of a new country, and a new way of life. To be in her company is very refreshing. I have found it so myself. She is completely without any self-consciousness; gay, good-tempered, bounding with vitality. Traditional taboos play no part in

Original designs by the Royal Dressmaker for the Queen's Younger Daughter

Norman Hartnell.

her make-up, and she treats Princess Margaret almost exactly as though she were one of her own girl friends from New York or the wilds of Arizona.

For instance, on one occasion, when a guest of Sharman's from the Embassy was going round the room saying good-bye and kissing her new English friends in a slightly exuberant fashion, she only just stopped herself at the last second from embracing the Princess, too.

"Look out," called Sharman from the canasta table at the other end of the room, "she will be calling you 'Maggie' next!"

The Princess can find such sallies amusing and relaxing after the inevitable formality of so much of her life. All the same, when the week-end guests retire to their rooms for the night, it is in the company of Caroline Scott, who almost takes the place of her lady-in-waiting at informal parties, that the Princess likes to brush her hair. Always, when she is staying away from home, she tells her maid not to wait up for her, and sometimes she will confess the next morning that she and Caroline gossiped for hours.

Of what? Well, although the wide Grecian forehead of Lord Dalkeith's sister is a frontier for the best feminine brain of any young member of her world whom I have met, I doubt very much whether it is of painting and painters—a subject of which Caroline Scott has considerable knowledge—that the two contemporaries chat away at midnight. Far more likely they discuss with mutual sympathy the predicament in which a member of the Buccleuch family finds himself at this moment.

Many months ago yet another paper—a French one this time!—had the temerity to inform its readers that at any moment now the King of England would be formally announcing the betrothal of his unmarried daughter to the Earl of Dalkeith.

Of course, from a worldly point of view it would be a most excellent match. Not only is Lord Dalkeith heir to the dukedom of Buccleuch, together with half a dozen houses and estates, but he will also be a very rich man one day. On the other side of the picture—the side that should matter even more—he gave a very good account of himself as a sailor in the war, and has worked extremely hard to become an equally good farmer in peace-time.

Johnny Dalkeith has flaming red hair, but is no rebel. He is serious and conservative by character, and enjoying country pursuits, goes to London as little as possible, for he hates city pavements or any hot-house atmosphere. His passion for horses the Princess shares—riding is the one form of outdoor exercise she really enjoys—and they have many other tastes in common, too. For example, they laugh at the same things. Not long ago, they went in a party to the latest Bob Hope film, and both enjoyed it equally.

In fact, there is only one drawback, though it is a considerable one to this "perfect match", this latest piece of match-making on the part of the romantically courageous or impertinent onlookers. (It depends on one's point of view.) The two people concerned are not in love. Very definitely not in love. And only when the Princess does find herself really and truly in love will she start thinking of getting married.

How can I be so sure that I dare to underline that last sentence? Of course, no one can be certain of the inmost workings of another human being's heart and mind. Moreover, it has happened many times in life that two young people have known each other for a long time as friends before they suddenly discover a miracle has happened and they have fallen in love with each other. Who knows. . .? That could quite as easily happen against a royal background as any other. Meanwhile I can only repeat what one of the Princess' really close friends said to me when I showed him a crop of these current rumours spread by gossip writers. "What utter nonsense," he exclaimed, with

considerable emphasis. "Why, the Princess and Johnny Dalkeith have been friends since their childhood. Old family friends, nothing more. The reason why the Princess sometimes stays at Drumlanrig with the Buccleuchs on her way to and from Balmoral is because Caroline asks her. People might just as well say she was going to marry one of the McEwen brothers because she stays there, too. Again friends of long standing. Of course, she is very fond of both James and Robin, but that is very different from marrying either of them. Why, it might just as well be suggested she was about to

Princess Margaret attends a Meet of the Beaufort Hunt

become engaged to Billy Wallace, just because she has happened to stay two years running at Beechwood for Goodwood. . . .

As it happens, both Billy Wallace and his mother, Mrs. Herbert Agar, are old friends of my own. I once motored from Arizona across America back to New York with Billy as my only companion. And I could not have wished for a more pleasant one. He possesses both charm and good manners, intelligence and a sense of humour. Nor has he allowed the accident of his birth and inheritance to build a sheet of thick glass between him and reality. On the contrary, he is interested in everyone and everything. As for his mother, Barbie Agar, she is a very wonderful person. At the beginning of the war she had five sons; now she has only one left, but she has never allowed her personal sorrows to cloud her genius for friendship, her passionate concern as to how the rest of the world lives, so that her home has become a happy meeting ground for many different kinds of folk.

For my own part, there is nowhere that I feel more at peace than at Beechwood, which looks on to Lavington Park, and was once Cardinal Manning's home. But there is nothing grand or imposing about it. Instead it nestles quietly against the Sussex Downs, with a great army of beech trees guarding the horizon, and a very pleasant, old-fashioned kind of garden in which one's hostess is always working at week-ends.

The Princess loves staying there because the atmosphere is so completely natural. Here she finds both spontaneity and privacy. If she wants, she can watch her young host playing polo at Cowdray Park in a setting that is incomparably English, or else she can join in the pirate croquet on the home lawn that is equally green. Always, too, there is good talk and intelligent company, for Billy's stepfather, Herbert Agar, the American historian, has one of the most brilliant of living minds.

"I like talking to him very much," the Princess told me, not knowing that only a few weeks before the author of *A Time for Greatness* had remarked: "Of all the young friends of his own age that Billy invites to the house, no girl is so easy to talk to, or better informed on a surprising number of subjects."

That assessment from a citizen of another country and very definitely another generation was worth keeping, I felt, for the end of this chapter.

Six .

IF half a dozen godparents were asked their opinion as to what one quality above all others they would like to give to any child, at its christening, so as to ensure its future happiness and success, it could hardly be expected that there would be universal agreement. For one might suggest charm rather than good looks, another a carefree disposition instead of a clever brain, a third steadfastness of character in preference to a plausible tongue.

Baron

Wearing her favourite ball dress on her twentieth birthday

Royal Tour in South Africa

The arrival at Cape Town

Nevertheless, all those six adult human beings might well finally agree that there remained one quality which has been known to take a great number of people a very long way in life. That quality is vitality, and it is one that the King's younger daughter possesses to such a marked degree that even her contemporaries find it hard not to flag sometimes before an evening's programme in her company comes at last to an end.

For instance, of all the parties given last summer, the one that will probably linger longest in the memory of those who were there was the ball given by Lord and Lady Leicester at Holkham for the coming out of their daughter Anne, and honoured by the presence of the King and Queen and Princess Margaret.

The Norfolk home of the Leicesters, with its noble façade that is a landmark throughout the county, owes much of its splendour to the influence of the famous early eighteenth-century architect, William Kent. The exquisitely proportioned hall is colonnaded, there is a library full of treasures, while on the evening of the party the historic beauty of the setting was greatly enhanced by the garden avenues that lead towards the great stone obelisks being floodlit until the dawn.

And until the dawn, long after her parents had gone to bed, the Princess went on dancing. Indeed, only when the band could

The Royal Family get ready to be photographed by their host, Field-Marshal Smuts, in the National Park, Natal

play no more, their heads drooping, and there were less than half a dozen couples left on the ballroom floor, did she reluctantly leave Holkham and allow herself to be driven back to Sandringham.

Even more lovely than the effects of the floodlighting were the natural hues of tha new day. So much so that the Princes described it as reminding her of one c the pictures by Paul Nash that her mothe possesses in her private collection. Howevei her appreciation of the landscape was onl

matched by her appetite for breakfast before she climbed the stairs to sleep for a few hours, still chattering eagerly to her own house-party of guests about the revels now ended.

One might have thought that by now she might have become slightly blasée, or even satiated by a succession of such parties, but the truth is the Princess goes to each ball as eagerly as Cinderella, though she pays no attention at all when the clock strikes midnight. For though her delight in dancing, whether it is a Scottish reel at a Highland ball, or the revived—and revised—version of the Charleston (that was once the passion of her Uncle David), springs quite naturally from her bubbling-over vitality, there is far more to her eager acceptance of dance invitations than that. The truth is, her love of dressing up and going out for the evening is part of her eagerness to meet new people, to see new faces and listen to new points of view, and wherever possible, without loss of royal dignity, to make new friends from other worlds than her own.

It is the same kind of eagerness that will take other girls of her age to the local palais de danse on a Saturday night, or to stay for a week in a Butlin camp. The impulse is perfectly natural and reasonable. Nor is it surprising that the Princess should sometimes long for similar freedom, similar opportunities for widening her circle of experience and of friendship. Nor is there any doubt at all that could she be anonymous for an evening in public, say, in the Winter Gardens Ballroom at Blackpool, her vitality, just as much as her disarmingly frail, porcelain prettiness, would keep her on the floor dancing every dance until Joe Loss's band played *God Save the King*.

For that, if nothing else, would bring the return of reality, and she would be compelled to remember that, though she had been born into an age far less conventional than its predecessors, the barriers that surround her own position are still impregnably high, whatever efforts she may make to break them down.

After all, any other girl in any other world can go out with any young man she chooses. The Princess can never do that, never go out alone with one person. There must always be at least four in the party, more often six or eight, to prevent any comment, any apparent preference for the company of one friend more than another.

Again, although she may ask her girl friends to visit her for tea or at cocktail time in her own apartments at the Palace, she will never invite any of her men friends unless she is certain there will be a dozen guests in the room. The nearest she can reach, in fact, to being on intimate terms with anyone, is to send them a letter in her own handwriting or to ring them up on the telephone in her sitting-room. That, at least, is a private conversation without eavesdroppers, and perhaps, on this account, she is often on the telephone by half-past nine in the morning. In turn, from that hour, her friends are at liberty to ring up the Palace and to ask to be put through to Her Royal Highness. And they know that the invitation that will please her most will be to see a new programme of the ballet, whatever company is performing at Covent Garden, or to pay a return visit to her favourite of all, *The Sleeping Beauty*.

The ballet has become the most popular of all entertainments today. In an age menaced by war clouds, bureaucracy-ridden and beset on every side by austerity, the combination of the music, the dancing and the *décor* undoubtedly possesses the power at once to soothe and to stimulate a multitude of troubled minds; further, to make every member of the vast audience believe that there is still magic and beauty in the world.

Certainly no member of any Covent Garden audience is more enrapt than the girl who is proud to number among her acquaintances today the greatest dancer in the world, Margot Fonteyn, and her

Cantering along the beach at East London

colleagues Frederick Ashton and Robert Helpmann.

Nor does the Princess ever tire of the thrill of going backstage to meet and congratulate the performers. To slip through the pass door gives her a sense of inward excitement, the same sensation as the fans have at the stage door waiting for autographs. Her own admiration is no less, and on one occasion the dancer who was playing the name part of *Hamlet* had not time even to wipe the perspiration from his face before he was bowing over the Princess' hand. "A pool started to form at our feet as questions were showered at me," David Paltenghi told me afterwards, "but the Princess did not seem to mind. . . ."

Of course not. Through these informal visits backstage she feels that she is getting nearer to a world as disciplined as her own, but in some ways infinitely freer and more exciting. So that after the performance is over she prefers not to go to one of the grand West End restaurants like *21* or

Signing the Golden Book at Port Elizabeth

Society, or *The Colony*, where she has danced on other occasions, but instead to a smaller, more intimate spot, like *La Belle Meunière* or *The White Tower*, both situated in a back street off Tottenham Court Road, and both famous for their delicious but unconservative cuisine.

Actually, her host is often a young Conservative M.P., Hugh Fraser. However, their friendship has nothing to do with politics, but is based on their mutual love of the ballet and the fact that he is often invited by her parents to stay at Balmoral. Indeed, the Princess is just as likely to be the guest of an ex-Balliol scholar, now in the publishing world, Mark Bonham Carter, who, in his turn, is a loyal Liberal. And the Princess makes it quite clear that she would be equally happy to sit next to an ardent Socialist at supper, provided they had other tastes in common, such as the Theatre. . . .

Mark Bonham Carter's grandfather was Mr. Asquith, and today his mother is not only one of the leaders of the Liberal Party, but recognized by all parties as being the best speaker of her sex on a public platform in England. In private conversation her son has inherited much of Lady Violet's brilliance, and although he is several years older than the Princess, he has become more and more her constant escort on those evenings when she is out "exploring".

Moreover, this war-time Guards officer, who made a thrilling escape from an Italian prison camp, has another gift apart altogether from his wit and his wisdom that must appeal to the Princess. He is far better than some at keeping unwanted publicity at bay. A problem which does not grow less as the Princess grows up. . . .

Now whenever this particular royal party, wishing to remain incognito, visits a restaurant like *The White Tower* or *La Belle Meunière*, the proprietor, of course, is informed in advance, and there is a table reserved in the quietest corner, but that is all. There is no extra fuss, no bowing or scraping, no ringing up of the newspapers, no whispering in the ear of neighbours. . . .

The Princess' detective remains discreetly outside. Her watchdog used to be Sergeant Green, and is now Sergeant Ashbrook. When Sergeant Green died the Princess lost a dear friend. She was devoted to him, and his sudden death was a great shock to someone so far only used to life. His place has been taken by a very pleasant-looking young man in a neat blue serge suit and a stiff white collar, who one would mistake, in the tube, for a stockbroker's clerk on his way to the City.

Only once when she had been out on her own were the services of the Princess' personal bodyguard needed. That was when an over-enterprising photographer, having followed the royal car from Covent Garden, disguised himself as a fellow diner and let off a flashlight in her face. A horrible experience for someone who was trying to forget for a few hours her inexorable destiny.

However, the picture was never developed. True, it was harmless, but there was a principle at stake. The detective dealt quietly but firmly with the intrusion and then returned to his vigil.

Sometimes, if she thinks she may be very late, the Princess wants to send away her car, but it is much more difficult for her to persuade her watchdog also to go home. Even if she sends him a message that she will be driven back to Buckingham Palace by one of the guests, he will stay behind to shadow her, following at a brief distance in a taxi or police car. Those are his orders; that is his responsibility.

And I feel it is, perhaps, my responsibility now to contradict what was a widely circulated story at the time, connected with the evening when the Princess had been present at a largish gathering of her friends at the restaurant in Chesterfield Street where the waiters always wear powdered wigs and silk knee-breeches.

The party was a happy one and broke up late. This encouraged one paper to hint strongly that the supper had been held to celebrate the imminent engagement of the Princess to Lord Dudley's son, Peter Ward, who was at that time sharing a house at Oxford with his contemporary, Billy Wallace, and is now learning the intricacies of the banking system in a City office.

As proof positive of the closeness of his relationship to the Princess, it was boldly announced that Peter drove her home alone from Chesterfield Street in his Bristol car, the twin of the one that Billy Wallace possesses. When in actual fact—and it is a fact—the Princess went home that night to Buckingham Palace in one of the royal cars.

However, even without that piece of "evidence"—now refuted by the Princess herself—the supper had been announced in advance as being a celebration one. So that would have been quite sufficient in itself for the usual crop of rumours to burst forth round the West End.

Of course, the rest of the party at *21* that night, knowing the truth, how they had been celebrating nothing more exciting than

the return into their midst of Billy from a visit to the States, were able to treat these stories of yet another "royal romance" with some amusement.

The joke, however, must have seemed considerably less funny to the protagonist concerned, who found himself pursued by news agencies to make a personal statement.

So I was not surprised, a day or two later, to meet Peter Ward looking harassed and unhappy. Still, at any rate, he could count on the Princess' support in his predicament, for she possesses a passionate sense of loyalty in her make-up. Indeed, once she has decided to make a friend of someone, she never wavers.

Perhaps her fairy godparents in their superior knowledge of the world, included that quality at her christening, as well as her immense vitality. At any rate, the spring is there, and though some of her close friends are not as fond of each other as she is of them all, she will never allow one word of criticism of any other member of the circle in her presence. And if it should still occur she is adamant in the other's defence.

All of which would suggest that the Princess has assimilated surprisingly early in life the fundamental axiom that if you desire to have many lasting friendships you yourself must always be a true friend . . . blow hot, blow cold.

Many have found it a virtue easier to praise than to practise. However, not everyone has been so fortunate as this King's daughter in the close-knit loyalties of her own home life. And it is of that side to her life, that rock of strength, that I shall try to draw a picture in the next chapter of this chronicle.

Seven

IT must be a curious sensation for someone to hear the proud, oft-reiterated cry that an Englishman's home is his castle when, as in Princess Margaret's case, two of her own five family homes are, in actual fact, real castles. What's more, if one of them, Balmoral, can be dismissed from the outside as an example of Scottish baronial Victorian architecture, the other, stretching back into the medieval mists, can truthfully claim to possess the most picturesque and dramatic exterior of almost any castle in Europe.

Indeed, when one gazes up the broad walk towards the towers and turrets of Windsor Castle, silhouetted against the tranquillity of an autumn twilight, one finds oneself forgetting that for part of each year it is the home of the King and his family, filled with life and week-end guests or parties for Ascot; one is only conscious instead of its past and its place in the tapestry of our history, and still very grateful for its outward show of impersonal strength.

Not surprisingly the Princess herself cannot forget that she was "evacuated" there during the war, playing her duets with her sister more loudly on the schoolroom piano to drown the sound of neighbouring gunfire. Even today, each time she glances out of the window, it is to see a sentry on the terrace, looking somehow so much more stern and uncompromising than the human replica of "toy soldiers" in their scarlet tunics and big black bearskins outside Buckingham Palace.

Nevertheless, she smiles, remembering how as a child evacuee she played pranks with those same Windsor Guards, on one occasion persuading her governess to touch off the alarum bell before breakfast, and on another creeping through the woods at nightfall, until she was challenged, when in her excitement she completely forgot the watchword and the poor flummoxed sentry had to shout out: "Your Royal Highness, who goes there?"

Today, when the Royal Family moves to Windsor each year for Easter, the Princess assured me that she recaptures with a sense of keen pleasure that feeling of security and strength that the solidity of the castle gave her first during the war years. "I always felt so absolutely safe," she says, though I would have thought myself that though the dungeons no longer house the Crown jewels in hat boxes (a war-time expediency), they are still very much there, and so is the feeling of the hungry generations treading the living down: a feeling captured most strongly in the series of paintings that the distinguished modern painter, John Piper, recently produced of the environs of the castle.

But thanks to the efforts of the Queen to banish the ghosts of the past, to break through precedence by placing a man of letters like Sir Osbert Sitwell on her right at dinner, to give a cocktail party at the end of each day's racing at Ascot, to have canasta tables set out after dinner in the white drawing-room, where once Queen Victoria used to receive Disraeli, much has

A fairy Princess meets a giant farmer in Swaziland

)een done to dispel the sense of formality, o much greater than at Buckingham Palace. Especially is this so when Princess Margaret persuades her parents' official guests, the foreign ambassadors and the cabinet ministers, to play her own favourite, 'The Game".

*   *   *

However, the Royal Family have another home at Windsor, a mile and a quarter from the Castle as the crow flies, and there is no doubt which Princess Margaret prefers. It is Royal Lodge every time. When one asks her why, she replies, with a faint shrug of her shoulders, as though no explanation was really needed, "Oh, we love it . . . because we were able to do things to it ourselves . . . you know . . . bit by bit."

They even hacked down all the undergrowth themselves, and at week-ends the King, wearing old flannels and a sweater, would produce most fearsome weapons of destruction, which would terrify the Queen, who could not be persuaded either to take part or to stay out of sight—and fear—indoors. Instead she just hovered, while everyone else plunged into the fray, herself filled with apprehension, like any other mother, that the children would cut off their thumbs with the saws, or worse befall.

A musical Princess watches a native girl perform in the Transvaal

With her sister in the Royal Procession at Ascot

"Oh, Lilibet, take care . . . oh, Margaret, do look where you are going."

Usually, when anyone is making a garden, they are glad enough to enlist any outside help they can muster. ("Yes, by all means come down and stay, but we shall expect you to *work*.") However, the family who spend as much time as they can at Royal Lodge were too grateful for their hide-out to barter one inch of undergrowth for their freedom. No one except the family themselves ever stayed at week-ends. Perhaps a rare invitation to a meal, but never to sleep. This was the one door marked "Private", ever since the Duke of York acquired the estate as a country home for his young family.

And though the children are now grown up, it is still the same today. Before Princess Elizabeth married she was encouraged to ask anyone she liked to Balmoral, and some of the same friends turn up, like Lord Carnarvon's heir, "Porchy", who is a first-class shot, and Lord Westmorland's brother, Julian Fane, who is rich in personal charm, and has had the privilege of escorting Princess Margaret in London to see one of his own plays performed. All the same, none even of her sister's closest friends, or her own, would expect an invitation to Royal Lodge.

On the other hand, each summer there is much speculation in certain circles as to who

With her aunt, Princess Royal, in the paddock at Epsom

will be fortunate enough to be summoned to Balmoral before the King comes south to Sandringham, in October, for the partridge shooting. Nor are the invitations issued months ahead, as for the Ascot house party, but sometimes, most informally, almost at the last moment. And no specified length of stay. So that after a week the guest wonders whether he will be reprieved for another day or two's sport in this Highland fastness, or whether he will have enough clean clothes to last out, when his hostess says, "Oh, you surely needn't go yet. . . ."

And no one wants to go. It may be in the nature of a royal command to stay, yet several of Princess Margaret's own guests have told me, with some emphasis, how completely at home they are made to feel at Balmoral, almost as if they were staying with their own relations instead of Royalty.

Although Princess Margaret will curtsey to her father, together with the other women present, when they leave the table after dinner, there is, in every way, a much less formal atmosphere at Balmoral than at that other royal castle in the south. The King is always here on holiday—and that happy knowledge colours the whole atmosphere— while the Queen's genius for home-making has triumphed over the bust of Prince Albert in the hall and the Landseer pictures, including the enormous one of Queen

Victoria setting off with the Prince Consort on ponies for a day's stalking, which still hangs over the piano in the drawing-room.

What the present mistress of Balmoral has done is to make everything seem so utterly in character, including the tartan carpets everywhere that one cannot imagine the house being furnished in any other style. Which, after all, is the ultimate test in all schemes of decoration. Moreover, the drawing-room has been transformed into a most comfortable sitting-room, in which the guests on their return from a day on the moors, or stalking in the hills, are encouraged to lean back and relax after a splendid tea. Potted shrimps and girdle cakes, game paste as delicious as *pâté*, spread richly on hot toast, heather honey, and scones tasting as only the Scottish folk can make them.

Fortunately there is never any need to apologize for one's appetite after a long day in the fresh air, and the Princess emphasizes how much of everyone's time is spent in the open air, until after tea the Queen loves to join the young people and play canasta with them right up to dinner-time. The stakes are never money ones, but instead the fun and skill of the game. In fact, the last meal of the day at Balmoral often has to be put back half an hour, because the game in which the Queen is playing *will* not finish, or because her younger daughter *will* keep everyone enthralled by her impromptu performance on the piano.

"Listen to Margaret," her mother will exclaim in mock horror, looking up from the table as her daughter gives one of her best imitations of an English night-club singer trying to pretend that she has been expensively imported from Broadway. Invariably an encore is demanded, to which her mother listens as happily as anyone else, especially if it is the Princess' own latest favourite, *Silver Dollar*.

*   *   *

Actually, although this American importation has suddenly become immensely popular with everyone, *Silver Dollar* isn't a new song. It was written over thirty years ago, at the time when King George V was still on the throne, and Queen Mary was not only hostess at Balmoral, but very much so, too, at Sandringham. Even today, although the whole family gather there at Christmas, it is the personality and the presence of the Queen Mother that seems to dominate every inch of the house, the gardens and the grounds, with their scented background of pine woods.

Thousands of sightseers visit the gardens every year, and stand enthralled at the splendour of the herbaceous border that is one hundred and forty yards long. But however many times they may return they will be unable to challenge the feat of memory of the Queen Mother, who never fails to make a complete peregrination with Mr. Cook, the head gardener, asking about almost every plant—and certainly every gap. "What happened to the delphiniums there last year, Mr. Cook?" she will ask, pointing with her parasol.

Mr. Cook, with his magnificent waxed moustache, is a great character. He and his bonny Scottish wife migrated north from Royal Lodge, and at first they were not sure how they would like this other home of their royal master, but today Mr. Cook shows you his carnation houses with pride and happiness.

It is here that he grows masses of the present Queen's favourite, that very pale pink carnation that looks like strawberry jam mixed with cream, but equally he never forgets to pack up large boxes to send to Marlborough House. "We always like to look after Queen Mary," he said with some emphasis.

I could clearly see what an immense admiration he had for Princess Margaret's grandmother. Indeed, he assured me that no matter how early he might be bicycling after breakfast down the road between the gardens and the King's house, whenever the Queen Mother was in residence he would always catch a glimpse of her upright figure at the morning-room window. Which reminded me of the occasion when Princess Margaret is supposed to have come into that room at twelve o'clock and, seeing her grandmother seated by the window, curtseyed to her. "I don't think we have met before this morning, Grandmama." At which the Queen Mother looked up from her embroidery and remarked, "*I* was downstairs at nine, Margaret."

I was too shy to ask the Princess directly how apocryphal that story was—but I have been assured since that it is—but when I mentioned Mr. Cook's name she exclaimed reminiscently, "Oh, he was so sweet to me. Last time we were at Sandringham he gave me a peach. You know how it is," she added, "when one was small, one was usually caught in the act of just taking one. . . ."

And now her eyes are smiling, too, as she goes on to speak of her love of the Norfolk countryside, which is somehow quite different from any other county in Britain. How different? Because of its untamed quality and the width of its skies, and, above all, she decided, because of that exquisite golden light which you can encounter there in the late afternoon, transforming the landscape, touching the tops of the pine trees with gold.

*   *   *

Somehow you never seem to see that degree of refracted light gilding the grey stone of Buckingham Palace. Inevitably it remains a cold façade, so cold that you may remember I found myself asking the Princess whether she did not ever feel lonely and shut off in her apartments at the top of the house, without her sister any longer to keep her company in the rooms next door. Whereupon she replied without a second's hesitation, "But this is my home."

And I was answered. Yet in my mind—I confess it freely—a doubt persisted about this palace which, of all her five homes, is the Princess' most permanent residence until that day when she will leave it, a bride; a doubt, as to its *liveable* quality, compared with the carefree days when the family were still living at No. 145 Piccadilly.

I remembered, for instance, how when the King first was compelled to assume his brother's crown, and move his family to the Palace, he encouraged the children to have their rocking-horse just outside the study where he had to sign a constant stream of State documents, so that he could still hear the friendly thumpety-thump of their close presence, on the other side of the door, and take reassurance.

But now I shall remember something else. I shall recall that night when the King was so very ill—far worse than was publicly admitted at the time—and his night nurse could not succeed in getting her patient off to sleep. And just as it was imperative that he should have no more drugs, so was it imperative that he should have some natural rest from the intense pain in his leg.

At last, after she had impotently watched him tossing from side to side, the Sister made a decision. She went and knocked on the Queen's door. At once the Queen got out of bed, put on a quilted dressing-gown, and without another word followed the other woman, in her uniform, back down the passage.

As soon as she entered the sick-room the Queen sat down beside the bed. She spoke to her husband gently and softly for a few moments, and then her voice died into the greater silence of the night. For he had closed his eyes, and after a few minutes his head turned on the pillow and he was asleep. Naturally and deeply asleep. But for a long time his consort continued to sit there.

Perhaps, as she sat there, she held communion with all the other women keeping a similar vigil beside their menfolk, or their children, in other homes that equally could become a palace stronghold or a castle. Perhaps she thought, too, of her own two daughters, and how fortunate they had been not to be brought up in a house the size of Buckingham Palace, but in a home where love always dwelt.

One will never know. But one thing is positive and certain. No one in the family is more conscious of her good fortune so far—not in having so *many* homes, but in having *such* homes—as this younger sister, whose portrait I am privileged to be painting in words.

Eight

ALL through the planning of this portrait I have found myself again and again recalling a remark Princess Margaret made once which has, I think, such an overriding significance that it will certainly bear repeating now. It was when, as you may remember, she exclaimed with a rueful smile, "The papers *will* turn 'Lilibet' into the dull one, so they have to make me 'gay'."

The more I try to paint in the background to this portrait, the more conscious I am that the Princess has a great deal of reason for that protest. Of course, in any family the lookers-on prefer to make point of the differences between two brothers, or sisters, rather than to emphasize the likenesses. Comparisons are always easier by contrast, and certainly there was a period in the adolescent growth of this younger sister when she was only too eager to emphasize the differences herself. But that happens in other families, too!

It was simply part of the growing pains that occur in every home, and many readers will have a sympathetic twinge at the thought of the schoolgirl of fourteen, chained to her classroom desk, looking out of the window and seeing her elder sister most efficiently driving through the courtyard gate in an army vehicle. How she longed to be at that wheel herself. No wonder she

Just behind the Princess is a close friend, Lady Caroline Scott

Princess Margaret leaves the British Embassy Church in Paris

cried out with all the misery of the world in her voice, "I have been born too late."

Just over four years too late, she meant. The difference in ages. One would think it was unnecessary to point out that difference, but in actual fact just because through reason of their birth the two Princesses, fro their earliest childhood, have been so insep arable, both in public and in private, tha right up until the morning when Lilibet wa married they still had breakfast together their schoolroom, it has become a kind habit to speak of them almost as though there was only a few months between them.

It's easy enough to see how that has happened. For so many years they shared the same pleasures and the same clothes. During the war, when coupons were scarce, Princess Margaret always had things passed on to her, and for a long time she didn't rebel. And then suddenly, when the family returned from their South African trip, it was different. She felt grown up. She must prove that she was grown up. "I won't wear any more of Lilibet's clothes," she said. And she hasn't.

As for her shoes, extremely conscious also of the difference in height between them, she began to insist on having higher and higher heels. One day, when they were trying on new styles together, her elder sister protested that surely she would find it very difficult to walk. "Don't worry," Margaret retorted, "I have to wear them. Not you."

Always the shoes of the younger sister. It started a long way back, though one was scarcely conscious of it in the beginning, except when something special happened. At that time early in the war when Lilibet

Here she visits the Hertford British Hospital in Paris

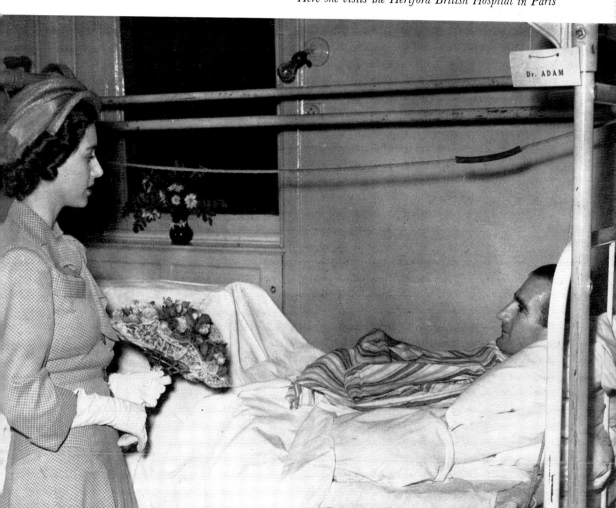

made her first broadcast, speaking so felicitously to other children evacuated like themselves, and then at the end spontaneously added a few words of her own, "Come on, Margaret, say good night, too."

By right of her seniority on such occasions the elder sister held the stage alone, though such was her nature she was as eager to share such a moment with her baby sister as she had been to give her the first ride on the pony which had taken pride among the presents for her seventh birthday.

Indeed, at all times it was her own desire, as much as her parents', that they should equally share their treats and their toys, though their reactions to their position in the public eye could, on occasion, be rather different. As on that day when a "confab" was being held as to how much they should charge for the seats at their own first pantomime in the Waterloo Chamber at Windsor.

Someone had suggested seven and sixpence for the front-row stalls. The Principal Boy was horrified. "We can't possibly charge as much as that," she exclaimed. "Nonsense," broke in the Principal Girl, "they'll pay anything to see us." When she noticed a certain reaction upon the faces round her, she added sweetly, "After all, it *is* for Mummie's Wool Fund."

I need hardly add that the seats were seven and sixpence. Nor that the "theatre" was equally as packed as the last time that the two leading performers had been able to see a London pantomime themselves, *Red Riding Hood* at Covent Garden. Dressed alike, as though they were twins, with equally engrossed expressions, they made a charming picture leaning forward in their box, eagerly joining together in the chorus, "How does the hen know the size of an egg cup?"

Fortunately at that time Princess Elizabeth did not know that she was to be the future Queen of England, nor the size of the career which irrevocably lay ahead of her. But from the moment that, as official heir-apparent, she was given her own standard and coat-of-arms, the difference between the two sisters became more than one of age or even temperament, it became one of destiny, too.

Whereupon the legend of the "dull one" and the "gay one" had its first seeds planted in the mind of the populace. Of course, the superficial differences were there. Lilibet was so meticulously tidy that sometimes she would get out of bed in the middle of the night to see if her shoes were in the proper place, whereas in those days her sister's dressing-table was always a hotch-potch. Again, they shared their love of horses, but not Margaret's love of staying up late!

But something infinitely more important was that Princess Margaret could marry a commoner if she chose, and the longer she took to choose the more delighted the world would be to have the chance of speculating about the ever-increasing number of "possibles", and backing their fancy. Whereas Princess Elizabeth must be married early to a suitable consort to make the succession safe. And when she dutifully produced a son first time, and her sister gaily remarked that of course from now she would be known as Charley's Aunt, as though the whole thing

*A charming picture by
Dorothy Wilding
of the Princess
at the age of seventeen*

83

was a wonderful joke, the seeds began to show above the ground.

The spectators (from a distance) did not appreciate that the younger sister really spoke with pride and loving delight in the happiness of the sister whom she adores. It seemed just like an amusing remark made on the spur of the moment, and she was known to have an amusing tongue that could be devastating when it chose. Nor do they remember now, in the tableau they have in their mind of the young responsible matron who had to cancel some of her autumn engagements last year because her doctors considered rightly that it was too soon after her second child's birth, that other picture which I shall always carry in my own memory.

It was an evening in July, warm and still, and there was a dance at Apsley House, the last private dance ever to be given in that house at Hyde Park Corner where came the first Duke of Wellington after his victories and history had been made. That night another kind of history was made, for at midnight we who were the guests of Lady Serena James heard as we danced beneath the candles in their great wrought sconces that an engagement had just been announced which might decide the succession to the throne for centuries.

But not for that reason was it so difficult to take one's eyes from the girl in the gold crinoline dress who went on dancing every dance almost until the end, and who might have been her younger sister that night. So radiant, so smiling, so utterly carefree. There had only been one dream for her, even

First holiday on her own. Arrival at Naples

Two pictures taken in Capri

since she had visited Dartmouth with her parents and a tall, fair boy like a young Viking had rowed out to sea after their yacht, waving them out of sight. Margaret might change her mind a dozen times, she had known right from the beginning, and now, like the fairy princess she truly looked that night, there was to be a happy ending, after all.

Dull? How utterly absurd. Serious and conscientious, and full of a sense of responsibility towards her destiny? Ah, that is another matter. And now I have another picture to add.

Very soon after their engagement was announced the young couple went north to Edinburgh, where Princess Elizabeth had a sheaf of engagements to fulfil. It was a very, very tight and exacting schedule and the first time that her fiancé had ever seen at first hand the ruthless demands of her destiny.

On the Thursday Princess Elizabeth was visiting a hospital in the afternoon, having already carried out a morning engagement, and been the official guest at a ball the night before. Half-way round the wards, as they were proceeding down a corridor, the guest of honour suddenly whispered to the elderly courtier who was escorting her, "I am so sorry, I feel rather faint . . . if you could keep everyone away just for a moment, I shall be quite all right again."

The Princess leant against a pillar at the end of the corridor, deathly pale. However, she refused utterly to cancel the rest of the timetable. A second later she said firmly, "I am ready to carry on now." Which she did.

An Italian boatman, Salvatore Ghiesa, helps the Princess on board at Sorrento

Then on the Friday evening it was all over and the Princess was at last back at Holyrood and going up the stairs to her own apartments, when the elderly courtier was halted in the hall by the sound of hurrying feet. He turned and there was his royal mistress with both hands outstretched. "Oh, I am so sorry, I was letting you go away without thanking you for all that you have done this week for me."

Dull? When Prince Philip returned south he summed it all up in his own way. "It's much tougher going than taking the watch and having to stay on, in a dirty sea, in the Atlantic for a week." It was his own baptism, and though he did not make the remark to his sister-in-law—who had scarcely yet had her own—if he had, she might well have replied:

"I know. I'm learning fast, too. Much faster than some people think. But I do wish they could give me a real job of my own. It's all right for you. You can go back to sea one day. But do you know what I envy most about Lilibet? Not her future destiny, but the comradeship she had when she was in the A.T.S. It was quite an ordeal for her because she was so shy. But I would have loved it, every minute of it.

"I was too young, of course. I missed the only chance I will ever have now of going into one of the Services, of getting away from being who I am for a bit. Now there doesn't seem anything definite for me to do except get married. And I don't want to have to settle down yet, for ever. At the same time, I certainly don't want to spend all my spare time being 'gay'."

Princess Margaret at a Florence theatre

Of course, that is an imaginary conversation. But the feeling behind it isn't. On the contrary, it is very real and very true. For had the Princess been a boy—and her elder sister a boy, too—then the fact that she was the younger child wouldn't have been a hindrance but an enormous advantage to her. She could have served for a time in the Navy, as her father did, or her uncle, the Duke of Kent.

For I have never forgotten an incident that happened at one moment in the war when the ship H.M.S. *Cumberland*, in which I was serving as a seaman, was on patrol in the Denmark Straits, between Iceland and Greenland. As you can imagine, it was very cold and very rough, and I was being very sick over the side one day when a stripey came alongside. He watched my misery not without sympathy for a time. Then he broke the silence.

"You know, in the last war, I was on this patrol in the *Collingwood* and, believe it or not, we had the present King on board as a snottie. Crikey, was he a bad sailor, too! In the end he was far worse than you, he was coughing up blood. But he was a great lad, and none of us will ever forget him."

Nor he them. Nor his younger daughter her longing to live down the false label that has been attached to her name. For she knows in her heart that even if she is not yet four years older than the label she has at any rate outgrown it, and only desires to be subjected to as severe a test in public duty as her elder sister, who once cried, "Oh, Mummie, I am so worried about Margaret . . ."

She does not worry any more.

After her visit to the Pope

VENICE

THE tastes of another human being are always interesting if only in contrast to one's own. But when that other human being happens to be the younger daughter of the King her personal likes and dislikes assume, if nothing else, a considerable curiosity value.

The Princess is very conscious of that herself. And anxious, therefore, that her private

POMPEII

inclinations should not be confused with her public interests. After all, if one wanted to sum them up in a sentence one could suggest that Mr. Winston Churchill's chief pre-delictions were painting, cigars, building walls and owning a racehorse. But his abiding interest would always remain the future of democracy.

Therefore it is with a certain sense of misgiving the Princess is aware that she has only to put on a pair of ankle-strap shoes for thousands of pairs to be sold all over th country. Indeed, on that occasion, withou realizing it, she was a considerable help t the manufacturers. For that experiment i shoe fashions had been something of failure until suddenly there was a pictur of the Princess wearing a pair hersel whereupon the country-wide sales situatio changed within an hour.

Again, so long as she chose to wea platform shoes, every other girl of her ag

Princess Margaret in the Mantovani Loggia of the Vatican accompanied by the British Minister to the Holy See

had to possess a pair also. It was the same with the teenage vogue that the Princess started for white accessories, a white hat, white gloves, white shoes and bag, such as she was wearing the day that she flew off on her first holiday abroad, that dream-like month she spent in Rome and Naples, Capri and Florence.

She has a passionate taste for travel, so far but tantalizingly whetted, and her whole face was transformed the day that she spoke

to me of that enchanted spring when she was permitted to make a shortened version of the Grand Tour. No wonder, the morning she flew off in a silver Viking of the King's Flight, that she wore touches of white everywhere, though she was criticized for doing so by one fashion editress on the grounds that anyone wishing to be considered really *soignée* would wear a completely dark ensemble that did not show the dust of travel.

It would be idle to pretend that there have not been other criticisms of the clothes that the Royal Family sometimes wear in public, but the great mistake that these critics make is in not being fully conscious of the exact reason why a certain dress happens to be worn on a certain occasion.

So I asked the Queen's dressmaker, who also has designed many things for her daughter, what conclusion he had now reached in regard to the dress problems and the dress taste of the Princess. Mr. Hartnell's answer was illuminating.

"Her Royal Highness knows exactly what she wants, and she misses nothing. I have never forgotten when I was making her first evening dress, just after the war. It was all white, and Her Royal Highness said to the fitter, 'Those short sleeves are too tight. It will be difficult for me to dance the rumba.' So, of course, they were widened. And bows!" Norman Hartnell threw up his hands in mock horror. "I have only to put a bow on a dress," he continued, "for it to be erased from the design at once. Her Royal Highness is extremely allergic to bows. Most girls of her age think that they make a dress more attractive, but increasingly the Princess' one desire is for simplicity and yet more simplicity. No addi-

Receiving a bouquet during the production of the film "The Magic Box"

tions, fussy or otherwise, of any kind. And, of course, she is absolutely right. With her wonderful complexion and brilliant colouring she needs the purest colours and the plainest designs, otherwise the final effect will be too overwhelming."

One morning, over a year ago now, when the Princess was having a fitting in her apartments at the Palace, she turned to her mother and asked whether she might not have at least one black evening dress. The Queen was doubtful. She felt the effect might be too sophisticated for a girl of nineteen, but Norman Hartnell added the weight of his own professional opinion, and in the end the final result was an immense success with everyone.

In his own private sitting-room at the top of his establishment in Bruton Street, Mr. Hartnell showed me the original sketch. The dress has a billowing skirt of black tulle and white marguerites cascading all over it. "It did not look a bit too old," he assured me. "In fact, I always think myself that the best time for any woman to start wearing black is when she is young and still has a naturally good complexion."

Since then Norman Hartnell has also been allowed to make a day outfit for the Princess in black, which was worn with a muff of white fur and a hat with ermine tails as trimming. What's more, she has worn this outfit in public as well as in private, thereby creating a precedent for royalty. For royalty is supposed never to appear in black, except when the Court is formally in mourning.

nd that is another important point which he critics of the bright pastel colours that the Queen and her daughter usually wear in public occasions do not appreciate.

Once again the Queen's dressmaker gave the last word on the subject when he said, If I am designing dresses either for Her Majesty or Her Royal Highness, I have to remember always that it is imperative that the clothes themselves should stand out as the centre of the picture, not only from five yards away, but perhaps from two or three hundred yards. Otherwise the spectators, waiting perhaps for hours in the rain to see the royal procession pass, will feel that they have been let down because they can scarcely tell from that distance which is Her Royal Highness."

The Princess' own favourite material is tie silk, and her favourite dress to date was the evening one in which she was photographed for her twentieth birthday. Originally it was created for the Princess to wear for the visit of the French President, but haplessly she was in bed with influenza, and walking through the Hartnell workrooms that week I saw the dress looking forlorn upon a dressmaker's dummy.

Princess Margaret inspects the Cadets at the Royal Naval College, Dartmouth

Another picture at the film studios at Boreham Wood

Two girls were working on the finishing touches to the stiff white satin skirt, sewing the pink roses to the corsage, and I stopped and asked them their names. One was Joyce Bone, whose home is at Stratford in the East End, and the other was Iris Russell, who lives at Kenton. And I remember asking them something else, too. Whether they did not sometimes feel . . . well . . . envious.

At once both the girls shook their heads. The more really beautiful a dress is for the Princess, they assured me, the more they enjoyed working on it. "You see," Iris went on, "we know we couldn't wear them ourselves. So it's like making dresses for my dolls, long ago."

Yes, but although the Princess has a 23-inch waist, there is nothing of the painted doll either about her appearance or her personality. For one of the Princess' strongest personal tastes is a taste for conversation. She enjoys a discussion upon any subject under the sun. And here again she has broken down the barriers that usually surround Royalty, the royal protocol that once did not permit a subject to lead the conversation, but only to answer questions. She encourages the atmosphere of a debating forum, and more than holds her own in any argument.

Incidentally, the Princess has one great hate—and that is any reference to her circle of friends as the "Margaret clan". She maintains—and she is clearly right in doing so—that she possesses a multitude of friends of different ages and interests. There is nothing clannish about her personal relations outside the Palace, because the motivating point of her philosophy of living is that she enjoys contact with many different worlds.

Again, her catholic mind shows itself, too, in the books that are strewn on the table in her sitting-room at the Palace. I myself saw that on top of the pile was Elizabeth Bowen's latest novel. But being so immensely feminine in her personal reactions, I was not surprised to hear that the Princess is equally an admirer of the works of Jane Austen.

One would think that the quality of femininity scarcely needed stressing, except that we live in an age of so-called sex equality, when many girls of the Princess' age enjoy wearing trousers, oblivious of the fact of how odd they appear from behind. The Princess herself wears jodhpurs for riding, and a hacking jacket with a masculine cut, but even then she compromises by adding a soft scarf—not a stock—at her throat. And she loves wearing scarves, tying them round her hair, like any other girl, when she is on holiday.

But unlike most girls today the Princess never wears ear-rings, and I have noticed with some interest that she never wears a ring either, while her hands, so far from being the scarlet claws that are fashionable today, have only very pale varnish on their nails. Again, although she uses lipstick and very light eye shadow, she uses no rouge in the daytime for the simple reason that she does not need to. Indeed, she is fortunate in possessing a thin and delicate skin through which the colour floods, giving her cheeks a warm glow that, close to, is immensely becoming.

If you did not know, you might imagine from that glowing skin that the Princess was a great advocate of outdoor sports. On the contrary. Although she does love riding just as much as her sister, and often swims in the

The Princess steps out

pool at Buckingham Palace which was blitzed and has now been repaired at last, her favourite joke in recent weeks has been a report in a London evening paper describing her as a tennis player above the average.

"I don't play at all," she admits, "nor golf, either." The Princess might have added that when she is staying away for a week-end, if the afternoon turns to rain and the party is kept indoors, she is perfectly happy to be allowed to sit at the piano and practise and improvise for hours. But not only "Boogie Woogie", she is just as fond of classical music, and never a day passes at Balmoral when the family are in residence, without the records of *Swan Lake* being put on the gramophone at her request.

Often her fellow guests will hear her singing down the corridors above their heads, singing to herself in her own room, singing in that true warm voice that could

"Public Nights Out," such as the Ballet Club's Bal

have earned her fame and fortune on the stage or radio had she been born into another world. One of her gifts—and one of her hobbies—is that she can listen to a piece of music over the radio, or even a selection of records—such as "Housewives' Choice," which she turns on every morning—and having heard any new tune once over the air, she will concentrate over it on the piano until she can play it with a professional a[...] herself.

It is the same when she goes to a show[...] and she loves her occasional visits to th[...] Palladium to see American stars, just as sh[...] enjoyed immensely her surprise visit on[...] evening to the Players' Theatre, ne[...] Charing Cross, where she happily joined i[...] singing the choruses of Victorian ballads.

where Her Royal Highness is accompanied by Lady Clark

On that occasion her companions drank beer, and she smoked one cigarette. Whereas her paternal grandmother at her age could only smoke in private, Queen Mary's granddaughter now occasionally smokes in public. The Queen Mother's only reaction to that was to suggest that the Princess in future should always use a holder.

The century moves on, and it is true that the Princess visited Danny Kaye in his dressing-room and he was invited by her parents to the Palace, but the rumours of a close friendship between them are an absurd exaggeration. He was simply one of the many people whom she has enjoyed meeting at different times, and to balance that leaning towards anything to do with the theatre, which is part of the dramatic

A night out for Cadet May

streak in her own nature, here is the other side of the picture.

Not long ago Lord Portal, who is very much a member of another generation, and certainly has nothing theatrical in his make-up, found himself sitting next to the Princess twice in the same week at different functions. "I thought the Princess would have had enough of me the first time," he confessed afterwards, "but on the second occasion she made me more than ever feel that I was the only person in the world at that moment."

Princess Margaret possesses that quality always, as many can witness, but she suffers from it, too, as when at a party a crooner will sing and afterwards the guest of honour will say a few polite pleasant words in praise of his performance. Two days later she reads in the paper that he is her favourite singer, and that she possesses every record he has ever made.

It is nonsense, of course. But what can she do? As I have already pointed out, she can never deny anything publicly, never answer back. "I wear what I'm told," she says with a disarming smile and a shrug of her shoulders. In a way, that is obviously untrue, but in a wider sense in its fullest implications that statement is immensely true.

For it means that the Princess has accepted her own fate. And though she secretly hopes and prays that her personal tastes may remain her own property, to pursue with freedom, she is today abundantly aware that her only interest from now on is to play her own particular part in strengthening the bonds that unite with mutual love and confidence the British Monarchy and the Empire.

Ten

AND now I come to the last chapter of the story, which in a way has not yet happened. Indeed, when I was about to start work on this portrait a mother within that same orbit exclaimed, "But the Princess hasn't had any life yet!"

It was a very natural reaction. Many other people, looking back across the extent of their own experience of life, may well have had the same one. Moreover, up to a point it was my own reaction when out of the blue my telephone rang in the hotel bedroom at Edinburgh where I was staying on holiday, and I was invited by the Editor of the *Sunday Dispatch* to undertake this biography. And since there has been so much speculation, I would like to stress that it was entirely Mr. Charles Eade's original idea.

I realized at once that it was a great honour, but also a great challenge. For was there sufficient material? More important still, could it be made to seem of sufficient general interest? I looked out of the window at the Castle ramparts towering above me, strong in history, and then I remembered something.

A tiny incident, if you like, but one that had left a deep impression on my own mind. The Princess had been staying with some friends of mine in the country. According to the papers it had been a typically glamorous week-end, divorced from reality as most of us know it. The chief guest had been photographed at the races and at a dance in a duke's house. There had been the usual report about her having bacon and eggs for breakfast in the dawn. . . .

But what the public never heard about was the private audience the Princess gave on Monday morning before she left again for her own home. She asked that all the people who had been roped in to help in the house during her visit could be assembled in the drawing-room. Then she shook hands with each of them, thanked them personally, and handed them an envelope on which, in her own handwriting, she had put their names. What was in the envelope is unimportant beside the fact—and it is a fact—that by her spontaneous gesture of kindly

The back belongs to the Hon. James Smit

The face belongs to the Hon. Peter Ward

courtesy she made that morning a dozen devoted followers for life.

You could say that I was the thirteenth—the convertee. For up till that time I had been rather inclined to take at its face value the public portrait of the Princess as it emerged from the pictures in the papers and the silly little paragraphs in the gossip columns. Though I had always had a sneaking suspicion at the back of my mind that the younger sister in the most popular family in our country was, through bad publicity, or bad luck—or perhaps a combination of both—being presented in quite the worst possible light to millions of people who through force of circumstances would never have the chance of setting eyes on her in real life, let alone speaking to her, or coming to know her in the way that her friends do.

After all, the Princess summed it up herself when she exclaimed in protest, "Some people seem to imagine that I spend all the afternoon lying on a sofa getting ready for the next party."

In actual fact, most afternoons she spends performing some public service and acquitting herself with the same sense of dignity and youthful seriousness as was so abundantly present when I watched her take her

The Highland Light Infantry give a party in Glasgow

place at that giant Girl Guides' rally outside Oxford. From now on there will be scarcely a day, except when she is at Balmoral, when the Princess will not find herself making similar public appearances. And one can only hope and pray that these appearances will be as greatly photographed and publicized as the other occasions, when like any normal girl of her age she enjoys being invited in a party to the theatre or out to dance.

In any case, it is only fair that I should stress again in this last chapter that it is Her Majesty the Queen herself who encourages the Princess to go out and about and enjoy herself, as freely as she can—for as long as she can. For, from her great experience, Her Majesty is so very conscious of how tremendously the weight of Royalty's public duties will press down and down upon her younger daughter in the years to come.

Inevitably, when the different chapters of this biography were first published in instalment form, I was the recipient of a multitude of letters, among them, as always in the mailbag of every writer, a tiny proportion of scurrilous and abusive ones— and I need hardly add, always anonymous, of course.

For instance, there was one I received from which out of pages of illiterate, incoherent boasting about what would happen when the "Revolution" occurred, one sentence caught my eye. This was the sentence. *"Princess Margaret will be drafted into industry."*

I suppose my correspondent meant a factory job. However, the joke is really on this "revolutionary" who had not the

Amsterdam was en fête *for Our Princess*

On this occasion the Marquess of Blandford is on The Princess' right

courage even to sign his name, because were Princess Margaret ever to find herself working in a factory, I have absolutely no doubt now that after the first few days of strangeness, such as any recruit feels in one of the Services, she would be a huge success, and the pet of the bench where she joined in the choruses of "Music While You Work". Men and women alike would come under her spell.

Her spell? Yes, I use that word quite deliberately. In any branch of the community into which she might have been born, given the same physical and mental equipment, the result would be the same. For she has gaiety and instinctive good manners—a rather rare combination among many of her contemporaries—wit and a very sweet smile, sparkling eyes and an extraordinarily nice nature. Indeed, considering how easy it would have been for her to have been completely spoiled, she has come through the process of growing up amazingly unscathed.

Now the chrysalis days are over she must be judged as an adult human being. But the more I delved into her present way of life and her present attitude to living, the more I heard to her advantage and nothing to her disrepute. Having a number of mutual friends, I was also considerably helped by very frank conversations with

On this occasion the Hon. Colin Tennant is on The Princess' left

them. For I was determined, when I accepted this commission, that though it was one which naturally intrigued me, I would not allow it to make me fall into the easy error of permitting my enthusiasm to gild the lily.

While, in regard to the Princess' own reactions, she made a comment as this portrait approached completion that I feel should be quoted now. "Of course, I am growing used to being written about," she told someone, "and accept it as inevitable. The thing that always worries me is my friends. I do hope they understand."

It was not possible to paint this portrait without many other faces appearing in the background, some shadowy, some etched in with care. Nor was it possible not to make some reference to the Princess' future destiny as a bride. Soon after these words appear in print it may well be that the Princess will make her final choice, despite the horoscope that was cast at her birth which asserted positively that this younger sister would not marry until she was twenty-four.

But whatever that final choice may be, one thing is certain. It will be a love match. Meanwhile, the central figure in this picture has one thought, and only one, uppermost in her mind. To prove to herself and to the world at large that in taking over many of her elder sister's public engagements last autumn she would succeed in proving herself such a splendid understudy that she would be swiftly and wholeheartedly accepted in her own right. As was her father at once from the moment that he was compelled to take his brother's place upon the throne.

How felicitous and fortunate that transference was came to me very strongly on one occasion during the war. I had gone as a guest to an investiture at the Palace at the invitation of a sergeant-pilot who was receiving the D.F.M. for his valour. Now it happened that among the many adventures in which he had been involved he had saved my life in an aerial battle over Stavanger against considerable odds, so that it was with deep feeling I watched his ginger hair reach the head of the line.

Afterwards I asked him what had impressed him most, and it was something that he could not get over at all. "You know," he kept on repeating, "after I had done my bow to the King, do you realize what he did? He bowed back."

From now on it will be the turn of Princess Margaret also to bow back to the cheering crowds as she passes on her way, performing her destined duties towards that greater family which embraces the whole British Empire of which her own family is not only the core but the figurehead.

Make no mistake. The Princess is fully aware that her life-work is only just beginning. Just as she is fully aware that she must *earn* the cheers, the homage, and one day, praise be, the adoration in which her grandmother, Queen Mary, is held. Moreover, she is equally aware that up to the present the acclamation she receives springs chiefly from the chance it provides the populace to show its love and gratitude towards her parents, who have themselves so wonderfully upheld the best traditions of our throne.

It is, of course, extremely unlikely that she herself will ever sit upon that throne; nevertheless, in the years to come when the Princess is following in her sister's and her mother's footsteps, setting her own example in that kind of family life which has always

Cecil Beaton

been the fundamental strength of our own country, I shall often recall once again the answer she gave and the look of devotion on her face when she was asked whether she did not ever long to be someone else, any girl of her own age, unknown, anonymous. To which she replied instantly, "I cannot imagine anything more wonderful than to be who I am."

Deliberately I have repeated those words, spoken in fealty and in gratitude, that I first quoted at the beginning of this book, because I cannot imagine myself a better end than that solemn spontaneous declaration for the one story which is now closing, the beginning of the other story which is still to be.